TEACHING TODAY

drawing

Norma Pitfield

Batsford Academic and Educational Ltd London

Acknowledgement

I am indebted to all the children and students I have taught and observed and in particular the students on the Post Graduate Course in Education, Art and Design Education for the sessions 1978/79 and 1979/80. Amongst those years were groups of students who chose to spend some time on their course looking in particular at the teaching of drawing. Their work and ideas have been particularly helpful to me.

Unfortunately all the children whose work has been photographed cannot be mentioned by name but thanks must go to the children of Winchmore School, Chase Boys School Enfield and Southgate School. These were the children who participated in our work in college. Without the interest and trouble taken to arrange visits by their teachers Bob de Quinn, Derek Rogers and Shirley Cottrell we would have been denied that opportunity.

However the drawings shown here and the ideas expressed in the book are derived from the work of hundreds of children and their teachers in dozens of schools.

Special thanks for help with the photography to Don Mackenzie, John Morgan and Tricia Ziff.

First published 1981

Typeset by Tek-art Ltd, London SE20
and printed in Great Britain by
R.J. Acford
Chichester, Sussex
for the publishers
Batsford Academic and Educational Ltd
an imprint of B T Batsford Ltd
4 Fitzhardinge Street
London W1H 0AH

ISBN 0 7134 3409 0

CONTENTS

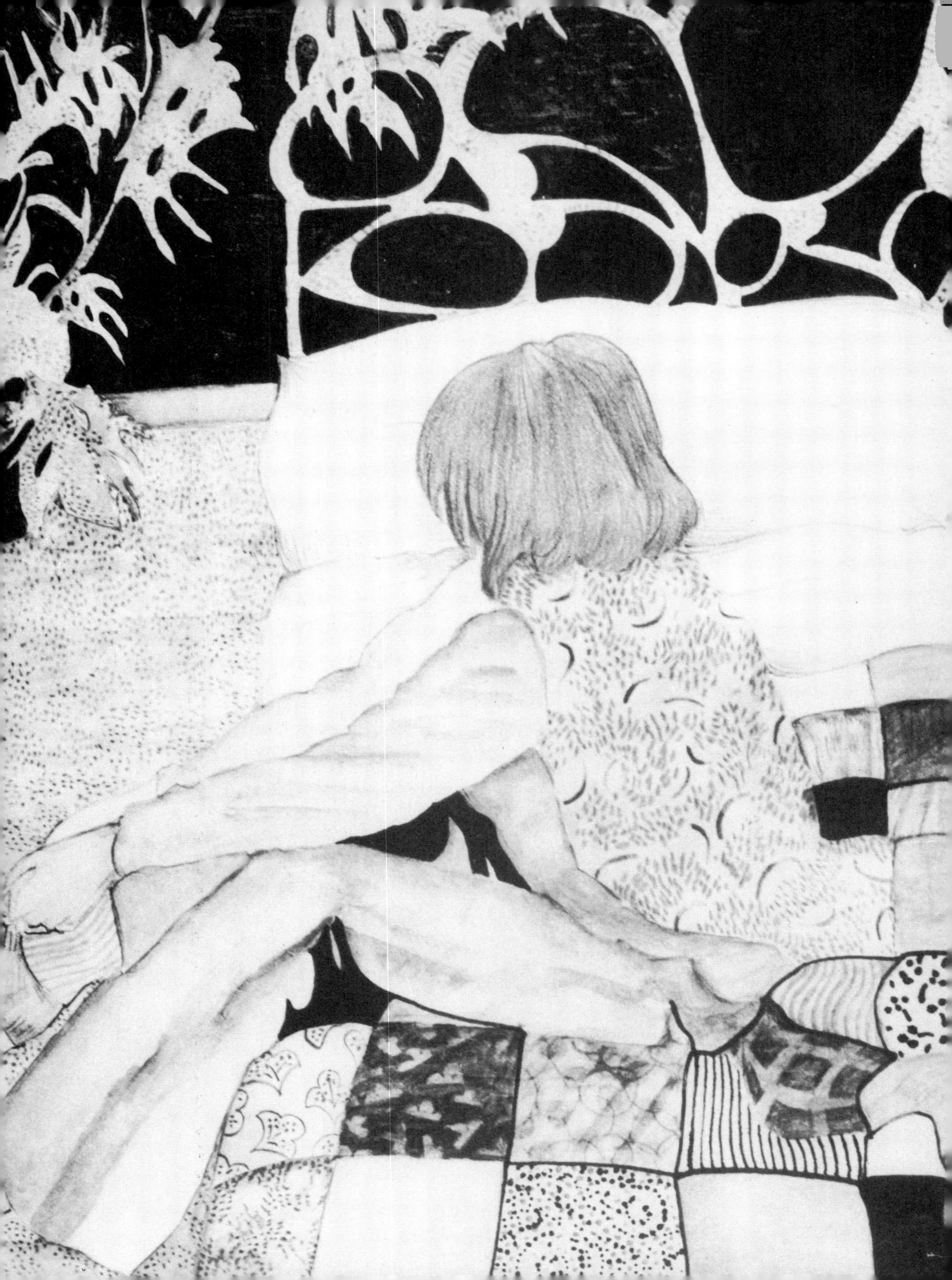

1 Setting the scene

I often yearn to draw, to feel that total absorption that making a drawing brings. At these times when no particular idea is at the forefront of my mind, I get out my various drawing materials in a methodical way, arranging them before me as a tempting feast. First a box of soft charcoal, the sticks enticingly wrapped in tissue, then a new box of precious conté crayons from France. The contents are the more exciting for being described in French, *ferme, moyen, tendres, très tendres, pierre noire, sanguine, sēpia* and *blanc*. The crayons are not yet sharpened and I look forward to carving to a point their perfect cylinders. Two knives wait in my bamboo box for this purpose, one a heavy stanley knife for the hard wood, the other a disposable craft knife to whittle away the points.

Along with the knives in the bamboo box are lead pencils, from the most fiercely hard 6H to the softest 6B, a collection of fibre and felt-tipped pens, a Chinese bamboo pen, and a set of flat carpenter's pencils, also several India rubbers. Next I open a box of coloured pencils, only recently a favourite drawing medium, another of pastel crayons and another of flat colour sticks. Finally I arrange a box of fine engineering draughting pens. These pens are such a pleasure to dismantle and clean, a preparatory ritual before

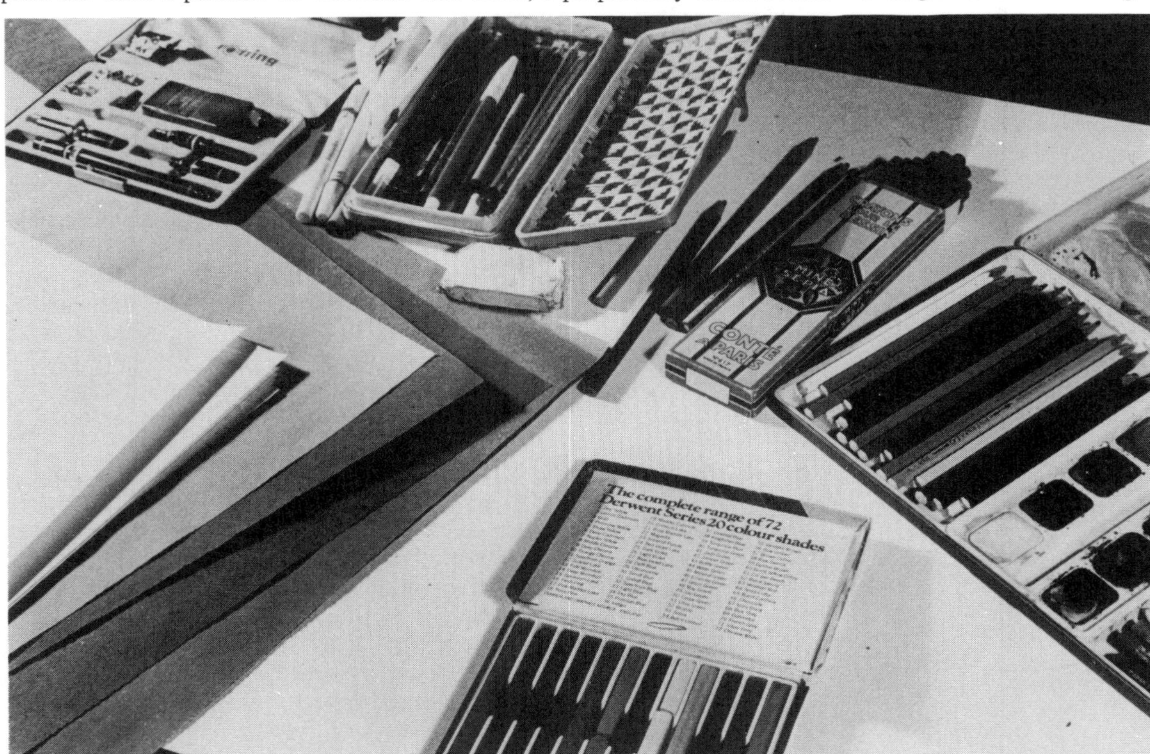

Setting the scene for drawing

drawing begins. These, plus a box of coloured inks, bright and translucent, a few fine brushes, my old school pen-holder and a card of nibs, complete a feast which never fails to whet my appetite.

The only problem that remains is how to chose from such a tempting array, and, having chosen, decide what surface to draw upon? Should it be hard, smooth paper or soft, textured or coloured? These sensuous pleasures are open to me but often denied to young people in schools where too frequently the choice is between a two or a three inch stub of HB pencil and either grey sugar paper or news-print, surely most unattractive combinations. Most of the types of drawing materials in my possession could be made available in schools. Some could be freely available, others given access to for particular tasks, or when concern and respect for materials have been demonstrated.

The qualities, traditional uses, potential and characteristics of particular materials are an important part of the inherent knowledge and understanding of any art or craft. Setting the scene for drawing includes that pleasurable anticipation of interaction with the various media of drawing. Walking into a carpenter's workshop, the sense of wood – its smell and feel – is strong, as is the awareness of the tools used to hold and form the material. Drawing workshops are seldom set up in such a specialised way, and yet the media and the tools of drawing are so various and rich that they need to be systematised like the various woods and the tools in the carpenter's workshop. How many young people are aware of the range of different types of card and paper or even of how they are manufactured? Knowledge of a range of papers by sight and touch and experience of drawing on some of them should surely be a normal experience for children receiving a comprehensive education in drawing?

Familiarity with the media and tools of drawing can best be gained by their use, but this experience can be supplemented by seeing others use unfamiliar tools and materials as well as by exposure to drawings made in a variety of ways. If we envisage an attractive, workable and provocative drawing scenario it must contain both activity and reference material. Such reference material can range from actual to reproduced examples of different types of drawing as well as drawings achieved through a range of media. Such examples could be shown alongside displays of drawing media and drawing papers. The categories of reference needed in the drawing environment are multifarious, objects to handle and study, photographs of images concerned with matters of interest from sport to technology, the third world, work, etc, collections of drawings from different cultures, collections of drawings used for a variety of purposes such as fashion designs, instructional diagrams, cartoons, maps – all should be available and collected by both teachers and students as an important part of the activity of the drawing studio.

Setting the scene for drawing is less demanding of space and less expensive than other Art, Design and Craft activities. The tools and the media are hand sized and mobile. The reference material can be used for activities other than drawing. But thought needs to be given to the physical working conditions for drawing. Clean, smooth, working surfaces, adaptable in height if possible and usable either flat or tilted in a good light would seem to be the minimal physical conditions. Drawing boards are a good investment, especially in a room used for a variety of activities other than drawing. Purpose-made drawing boards are very expensive, though pleasing in themselves. Improvised drawing boards can easily be made, given time and energy. Soft board is relatively inexpensive, easy to cut into standard quarter, half

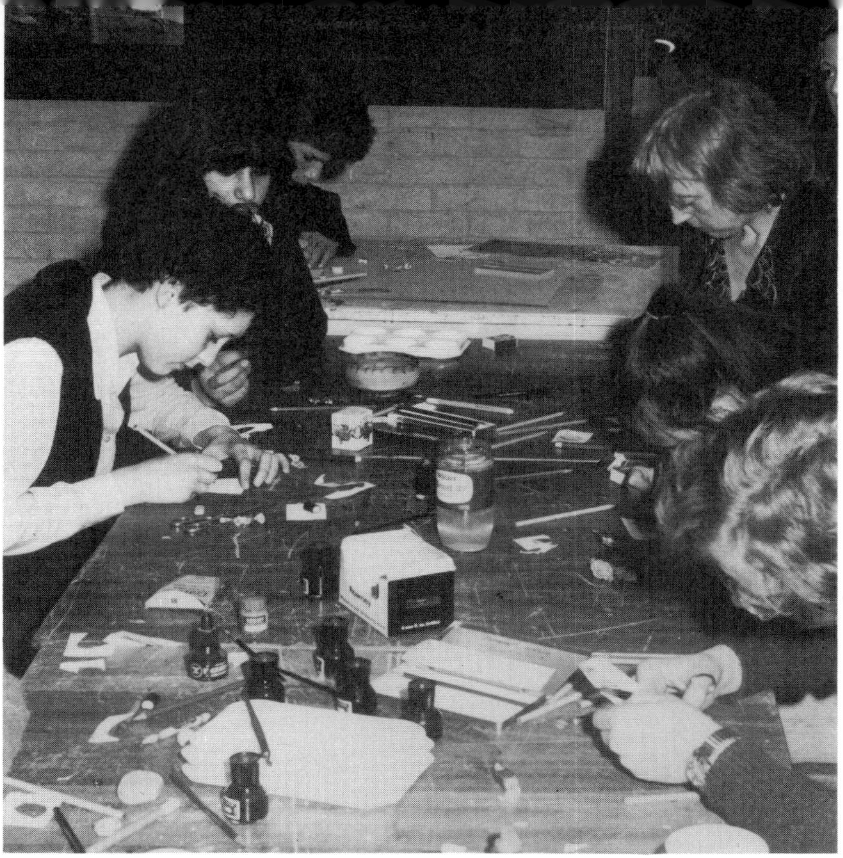

Drawing together. Children and teachers on the 'sweets project' mentioned later

or full Imperial. It has the advantage of being lightweight and the surface can be bonded by two or three coats of size or diluted PVA glue. Off-cuts of other woods, such as block board and hard board, can often be bought cheaply but have disadvantages of weight (block) or warping (hardboard).

Expense is a constant consideration in most art departments. If funds can only run to sugar paper, white is preferable to grey. Sets of every type of drawing material cannot be bought for every child, but as full a range of media as possible should be provided. If such a range is not available how can the relationship between mark and tool be shown? Unless every person can have the opportunity of experimenting at least once with every type of mark making instrument how can any kind of informed personal choice be made? Care and respect for these precious resources can be shown by students as well as by teachers.

Setting the scene for drawing is in itself a creative act. Care in making the working place right suggests care for the activity itself. In such a place the tools and materials of the craft are lovingly and logically evident, also working conditions are comfortable and flexible for each individual, a rich store of references are available which enable drawing activity rather than prescribing how it should be and, very importantly, adequate arrangements are made to store both finished and unfinished work carefully. The scene is therefore full of signals that valued, interesting and meaningful activity is possible there.

Defining drawing

What makes drawing different from other forms of Art, Craft and Design? In 25 years I have only once been asked this question, at an interview for an art teaching post. I was angry at the time – for some reason it seemed an

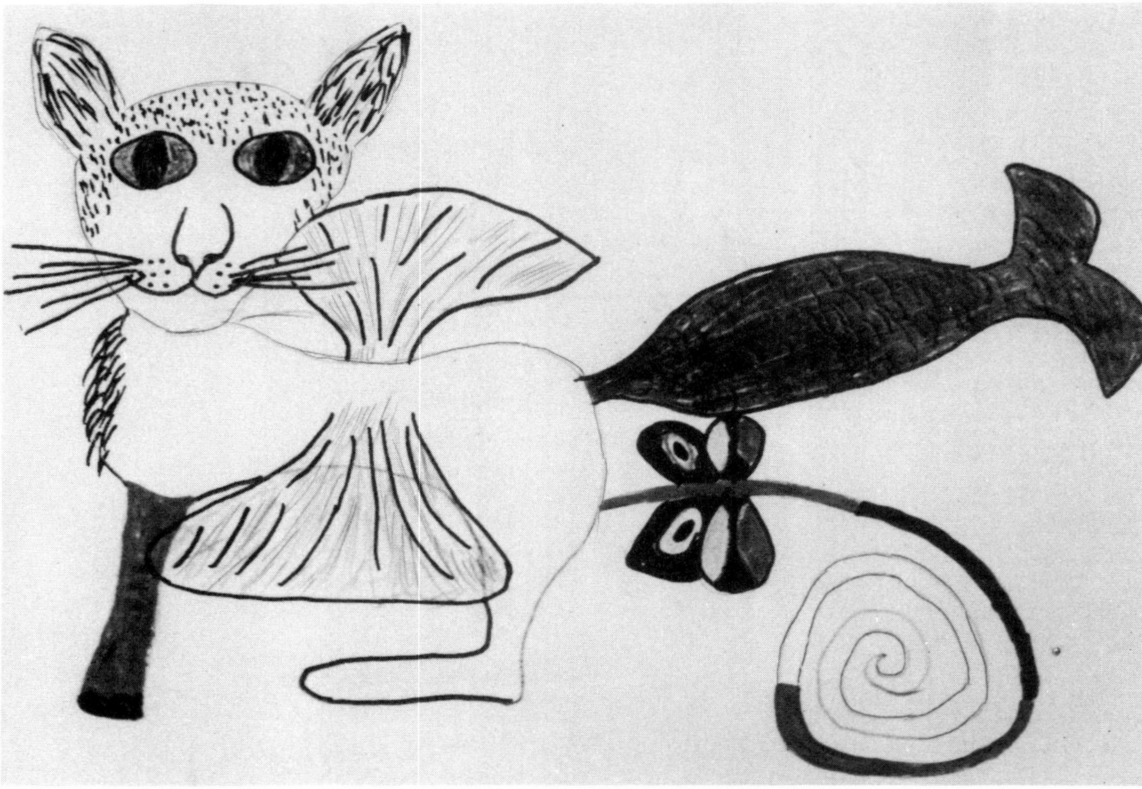

The children were asked to make a drawing of an animal, real or imagined. These drawings were put into a lucky dip and pairs of children then extracted two drawings and were asked to draw individually the offspring they imagined would be the result of the mating of the two animals drawn. This is a literal interpretation of the exercise.

unfair question. But now it seems perfectly reasonable though still a difficult one to answer. Is drawing defined by its forms or its content? Obviously drawing has subject matter in common with painting, graphics, sculpture. Is it in its forms that it differs from other aspects of art?

Drawing deals with illusions. On a flat surface it creates images which suggest shape, volume, space, movement, time, surface quality, qualities of light. Drawings can engage our feelings by suggesting evil, terror, disquiet, violence, pity, compassion, nobility, tenderness. Drawings can confirm our beliefs, they can also change them. Logic, computation and reasoning may result in drawing or arise from our study of a drawing. Pleasure, fantasy, imagining or arguing can all be stimulated by drawing.

All this can be achieved through marks made on a flat surface by an instrument held in the hand. Can drawing therefore be defined by the media it employs or as marks made by certain implements? Some would define drawing as the use of linear tools, that is those tools which create outline and tone by line. This definition would include pencil, pen, various crayons (dry colour such as pastel, oil pastel, conté), charcoal, in fact any medium which does not rely on the addition of water or any other solvent. But this would exclude the use of the etcher's stylus, the wood engraver's tools, the Japanese and Chinese brush, and thus image making where there is either the addition of a solvent or the intermediary of a printing technique.

I would prefer to define drawing as images where the gesture of the artist is apparent, where colour may or may not be a component and where a tool or instrument of some kind is used, whether it be the artist's finger or some other delineating instrument which could be wet, dry, soft or hard.

What distinguishes this definition of drawing from painting? Painting would seem to be primarily concerned with achieving shape, volume, space movement, time and the emotive aspects of the image through colour. Drawing can create these illusions without the use of colour.

Drawing as seeing

For a number of years I taught drawing to students described as 'mature', being between 25 and 50 years of age. More significant than their age was the fact that few of them had any protracted art experience, and fewer still had any confidence in their ability to draw. 'I'm afraid I can't draw', they would say courteously. They were brave, however, and hard working; even so I had some inkling as to how vulnerable and exposed they felt to be engaged in the very public act of drawing. Instinctively I knew that I needed to help these students to enjoy a strong sense response both to the media they were using and to the source material of their drawings. I devised a number of events to this end, often in the form of games, dramas, collections or expeditions, as a way into the drawing. Many of these students eventually produced remarkable work, but their comments at the end of the course revealed that something else had happened. They said, 'I'd never noticed colour and the feel and pattern of things before. Landscape I liked of course, usually reminiscent of holidays and that kind of thing, mountains, certain parts of the coast and so on. But now I can see pattern and meanings in everything. I notice and enjoy places and things I used to ignore, from the walls of my house, to the greengrocer's, to the rubbish dump.' Their perceptions had been heightened both to the formal qualities of colour and pattern, and to the personal and social meanings of the world they inhabited.

A central concern in the teaching of drawing is that it both depends upon and develops the perceptions. A common assumption is that drawing is mostly concerned with sight. I would question this emphasis. We experience the world by standing in it, sitting and lying on it, running, walking, cycling, driving through it. We experience the world through time and space; we touch it, we caress it, we grip, move and place objects in it according to their use, colour, weight, size and shape. Imagine moving house. Packing china would demand a different technique from packing cushions or blankets. The drawing of these objects would require an equally differentiated identification and interpretation.

Expectations, confidence, previous experience, the skills that we have affect our relationship to events. If I've been involved in an accident, that experience will strongly affect any drawing of an accident I should later wish to make. Without such experience my drawing would have to rely for its imagery on my fears and fantasies, which in turn would emanate from information and perceptions about accidents gained from verbal descriptions and media representations. Such perceptions, whether first or second hand, are stored. If this memory bank cannot adequately feed our imagination, then new ways are sought to acquire new perceptions on which to base images.

The teaching of drawing is concerned with seeing and sensing at every stage. First, students need to be helped to open themselves to their perceptions through looking, touching, listening and realising their spatial relationship with objects, places and events (the kinaesthetic sense). Then students need to be trained to store their perceptions in the memory, and to constantly replenish this store by developing curiosity as to the nature of things. The pleasure to be gained through, and thus the motivation to use, all the materials of drawing can be promoted through access to them. There is

Two disturbing drawn images
by 13/14-year-olds
based on the same input
as the previous drawing

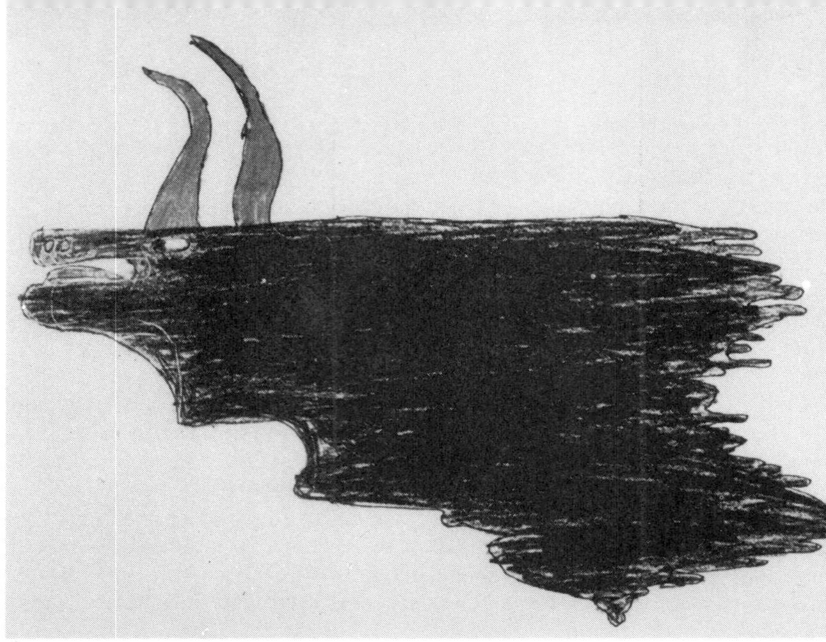

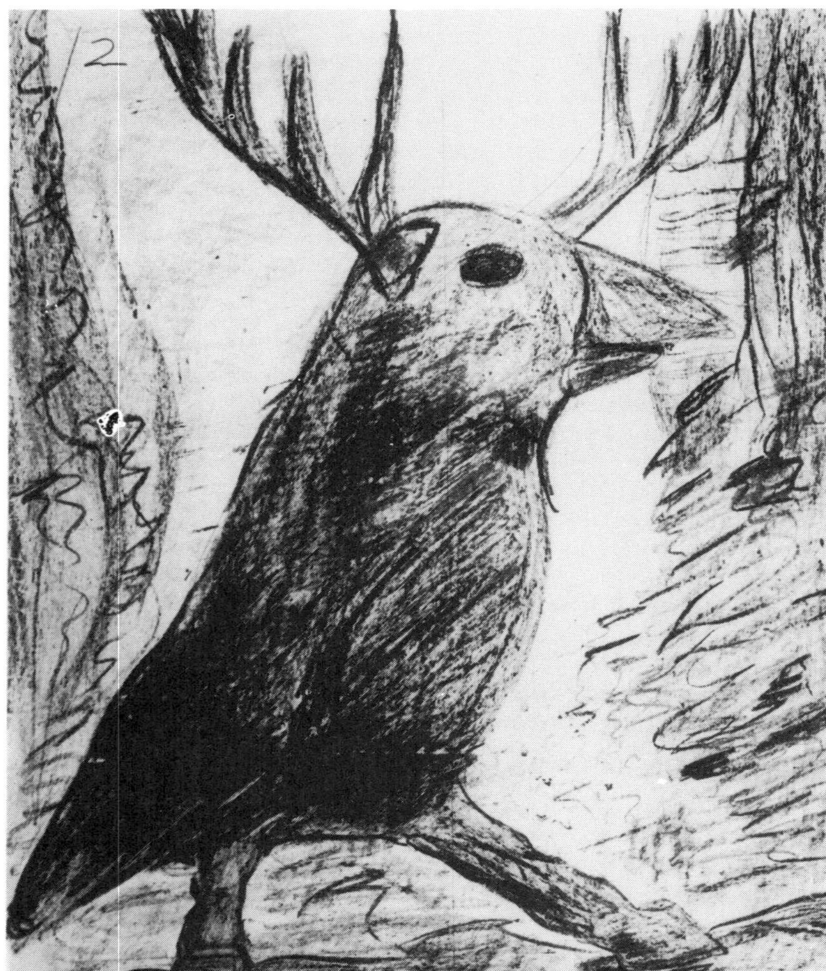

another important perception to be taught relating to the media of drawing and that is the relationship between the sensed qualities of these media and the images to be realised in the drawing. Whether the image to be drawn is from observation or from memory or imagination there will be sense qualities of softness and hardness, translucency or opacity, and so on; the materials of drawing have the same qualities and both the marrying of image and media, or of personality (of the artist) and medium is an important aspect of drawing that should be drawn attention to, both by example and by practice.

This personalising of perception should extend to the tasks offered in schools. Too often what is offered is a rather remote, observer's point of view. Objects and people are set up in a way in which the only perceptual relationship possible is a distant one. The framed moment of time in the middle distance is not universally the most enthralling one. A more intimate perceptual view can be more stimulating by being more immediate. Thus to vary the perception demanded by the task to looking up to, down on, through, to demand touch, smell and other sensations, may not only stimulate perceptual responses but also enlarge and enrich what already exists.

The universality of drawing

If we look at the drawings of twentieth century artists in any Museum of Modern Art, then go down the road and look at the drawing of people from a variety of cultures in the Anthropological Museum we can recognise two things, that drawing represents a common mode of communication irreplacable by any other and that there are a multitude of ways of drawing.

Ways of drawing may be linked to cultural or national traditions. Compare an Australian Aboriginal drawing of water with that of a Japanese artist, a Persian miniaturist, a Victorian watercolourist, a Seurat or a Social Realist painter. The obvious differences would be due to the technology available (in terms of materials, etc) but also to the history of the people involved and the function of drawing within that culture. The ways of depicting time, space, movement and volume in the drawing would derive from a communication system worked out by groups of individuals who at some point in time accepted a common visual system. From that point onwards the artist adhering to this system would be rewarded as functioning fluently and effectively. Thus traditions are formed and refined, or changed and jettisoned when they no longer serve a real purpose.

Do teachers attempt to define and explain the cultural tradition within which they operate? Do they attempt to enable their pupils to draw effectively within a given tradition? Do they at the same time demostrate that there are other equally effective drawing systems? If teachers are living and working in a 'multicultural' situation are they justified in giving precedents to any one system? We seem to live in a world which regards the Western European drawing tradition as sacrosanct, but do the images around us bear this out? The drawing used in cartoons, in diagrams and in instructions is often based on a system other than that of linear perspective and academic tradition. Our pupils are often able to read and understand a whole range of visual systems. Through the 'media explosion' the imagery of many cultures has been made familiar.

It is also now perfectly possible that many pupils will be more familiar with a drawing system different to that of their teacher. Their system may even be highly valued by the teacher though not by people in general, a familiar fate to those in cultural minorities. This situation has potential for the teacher of drawing. There is the opportunity both to teach students how to read different types of drawings with maximum fluency, and draw with equal flexibility through the experience of using a variety of systems: at the point when the student has enough knowledge to understand when one system is more effective than another for a particular purpose, a very sophisticated stage in learning to draw will have been reached.

Every adolescent has already passed through many different 'ways' of drawing. From early infancy strategies for drawing space, time and objects will have differed. Space will have been depicted in X-ray fashion with interiors and exteriors of people, places, objects depicted within one image. At another time space will be shown in plan and in elevation at the same time. A sequence of events will be depicted in one drawing as in a medieval wall painting. The importance of personages will be conveyed either through placement in the picture space or through the device of difference in scale. All these are honoured traditions in the art of various cultures and at various periods in history, as well as being familiar systems in the drawing of young children.

In spite of their own recent history, or indeed of their present drawing devices, many adolescents seem scornful and dismissive of anything other than linear perspective and straight forward representational work. Why do their aspirations seem to be so limited? Adolescence at its most banal demands conformity, at its best it asks for recognition of difference. The teaching of drawing should measure up to the latter, by giving the experience of many types of drawing, by discussion and by dialogue, and by creating an atmosphere of interest and curiosity in this universal human activity, as well as in the individual work of every pupil. Without the serious consideration of each other's work and the realisation that one drawing problem may be solved in a variety of equally valid ways, adolescents may be forgiven for assuming that their drawings must conform to an outside set of values.

The urge to draw

Most people respond and relate very strongly to drawing. Over the last decade public exhibitions of drawing have been particularly popular. Why should this be so? Is it because drawings bear the unmistakable stamp of the gesture, the personal and individual insight to which we can all readily respond? Drawings are intimate and direct, often they bear the imprint of second and third thoughts. Frequently they are not worked to the point where their manufacture is mysterious and impersonal.

The urge to draw is evident in most human groups, moreover the infant engages itself at a very early age in making marks. These early marks may seem to be random or accidental but the mark as evidence of exploration quickly becomes a way of exploration in its own right.

If we are to define the making of marks upon a surface which have meaning for the maker and for some, if not all, others as the essence of drawing, then it would seem that people from all cultures need this form of communication. Such mark making seems to stir a memory of an earlier impulse which was satisfying, meaningful and pleasurable. All cultural groups use drawing in some form as a way of thought and communication. Most groups evolve highly complex and systematic drawing styles which often have to conform to strictly enforced taboos, such as that against the depiction of the human form. The Western European tradition has depended upon a drawing system for creating the illusion of space through linear perspective which has persisted in spite of the Modern Movement. These traditions and styles while persistent are not inflexible. One strength of Western European art has been its reverence for individualism. This reverence has been a strong force in art education in this century, as well as producing a remarkably rich and rapid evolution in art styles and ideas.

All drawing has a common beginning. At the age of 18 months babies have the muscular control to make deliberate marks. From then on they engage in increasingly complex acts of drawing. The first mark must seem magical. No wonder, for it has awe inspiring consequences. Once that mark is recognised, perceived as being the result of one's own actions, a new universe immediately becomes available. Drawing, that tool of the exploration of reality, of fantasy and of the imagination, can express ideas from the most simple to the most complex and elaborate. Drawing can play with ideas in the most outrageous way. It can take risks with ideas, dreams, fantasies and fears. It can experiment with the limits of our experience, make new discoveries, propose new links, shock, delight, sooth, make for change.

Drawing is powerful.

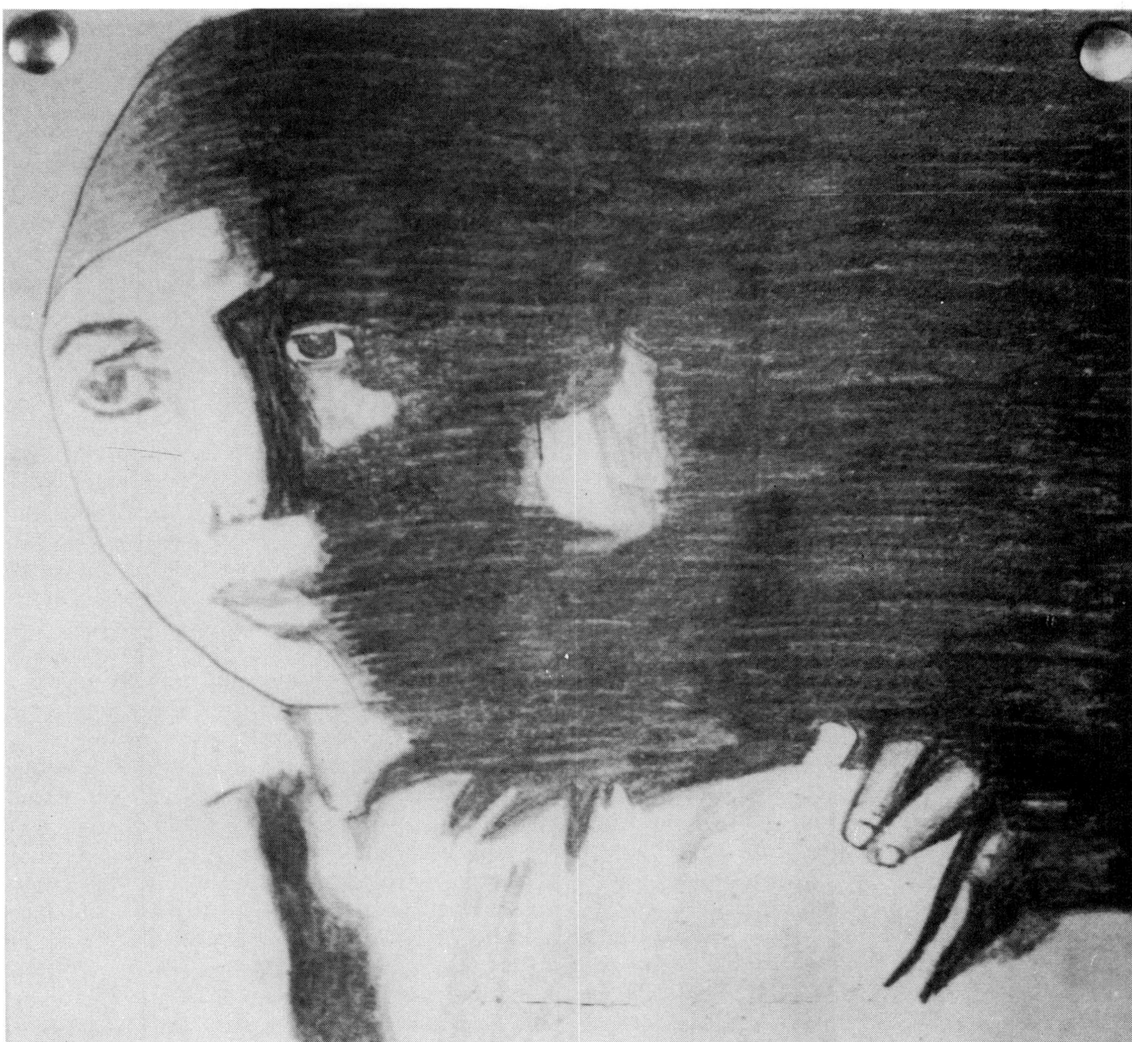

2 The uses of drawing

Adolescents often ask 'What use is drawing to me?', seldom 'What are the uses of drawing?'. A group to whom this question was posed recently were puzzled and unsure. 'Well drawings are like pictures, but without colour' was one reply, an attempt at a description, not a function. Others did understand the distinction. 'Drawings are useful because they help you with your painting', 'Drawings are useful because they can give you pleasure and remind you of things', 'Drawings can help you get the shape of things', 'Drawings are useless!' On the whole these were not particularly enlightened responses but they hinted at some of the functions of drawing.

Such hesitancy in defining the functions of drawing is surprising considering how frequently children are asked to draw. Next to writing it is probably the most common school activity. Illustrations, maps, plans and diagrams are required in many subjects. History, geography, science, English and modern language teachers expect children to use their drawing skills.

I remember as a young teacher being asked by a geography teacher why it was that she had to teach the children how to sharpen pencils properly, lay out the work pleasingly and neatly and so on. I was confused by these question and had two rather contradictory feelings. The first was that it was not my job to teach children 'that kind of drawing'. The second was irritation that children I knew to be careful, skilled workers in my lessons didn't apply their capabilities in another context, irrationally I felt they had let me down. It took some years to work out any connection between or resolution of my reactions.

My belief about teaching was, admittedly, at that time a narrow one. I thought my function was primarily to enable children to 'express' themselves through drawing and painting. It was a view based on a superficial reading of Marion Richardson's educational ideas, a 'self expressive' approach to art education. My reverence for the originality of the imagery of children blinded me to their limited range and lack of flexibility. I firmly believed that to draw attention to lack of skill would be inhibiting, even damaging. My approach was one often adhered to in colleges of art, that when the need to master a skill arose, then there would be the motivation to learn it and I would attempt to teach it. In classes of 25 or more such needs were often impossible to identify, and so diverse that they were equally impossible to deal with. When teaching other art activities such as pottery or printing, acknowledged as craft based, I quickly learned that such an open ended approach led nowhere. I therefore prepared programmes which structured the work so as to introduce skills in a logical sequence. Time was given for practice and application to a number of ideas. Originality did not suffer. Indeed with greater competence came more confidence. With more confidence, more experimentation and real personal expression was the result.

It took a little longer to see that such a teaching procedure in drawing was more logical and satisfying for the children and for me. How to apply drawing skills to a variety of functions was a more difficult teaching challenge. Secondary and Higher Education is traditionally compartmentalised into subjects taught by specialists. These specialists are usually concerned with the transmission of a body of knowledge, theoretical and practical, rather than with the social meanings of their subjects, or the relationship with other subjects. The results of this tradition are curious. A recent graduate in social anthropology had never been required in her course to look at a single art artefact, nor at the time had she recognised the need to. This strikes me as absurd. It is equally absurd to compartmentalise drawing as unconnected to anthropology, history, sociology, mathematics, technology, science or language. Drawing preceded written language and formed its scripts; much historical evidence is derived from drawing; some mathematical principles can only be expressed through drawing, as some drawing depends upon mathematical principles; technological innovations and engineering plans need drawing in order to be communicated. Scientists record their discoveries through drawing, geographers draw sections and maps to express structure and space.

Surely a function of teaching drawing is to demonstrate that drawing has applications beyond the art lesson? This is not to deny drawing as an art. Rather it is a claim for the strength of art. Art and drawing are not only aesthetic. The ability of the artist to symbolise and abstract has direct relevance to other forms of knowing.

The children's comments above indicate that many are unconvinced of the usefulness of drawing. The credibility of drawing must be identifiable. Through the teaching of it we have to ensure that personal gratification and self knowledge result, and we need to show that vocational application extends beyond that of the artist and designer. Credibility will also come through a realisation of all the functions of drawing as a unique and powerful form of communication.

Art functions differently in different societies. Art education must operate within, but not enclosed by, the culture in which it exists. It should recognise the many ethnic and social groups from which pupils come. It must also recognise the future life styles open to these pupils. Art education can help inform pupils as to work and leisure possibilities. One of the functions of art education is to show the connection between the mastery of the practice, and the understanding of the functions of drawing, and their future lives.

What are these functions of drawing, and how are they to be taught? All drawing must primarily be taught through practice, and so a drawing syllabus which aims to demonstrate these various functions would make the function of the drawing in hand apparent at all times. Drawing needs its models, the concepts behind the functions of drawings need illustrating. Making available numerous appropriate examples of drawing is thus an important provision. These illustrations would help to categorise the functions and applications of drawing.

There must be many ways in which categorisation of the *functions* of drawing can be made. What follows is one way and open to modification. It is a model which has proved helpful in devising drawing projects for the secondary age range. It has four categories, drawing as preparation, drawing as designing, drawing as information and drawing as personal statement.

Drawing as preparation

Whatever its application, drawing is tangible thought. When used as preparation for imagery it is a particular kind of tangible thinking.

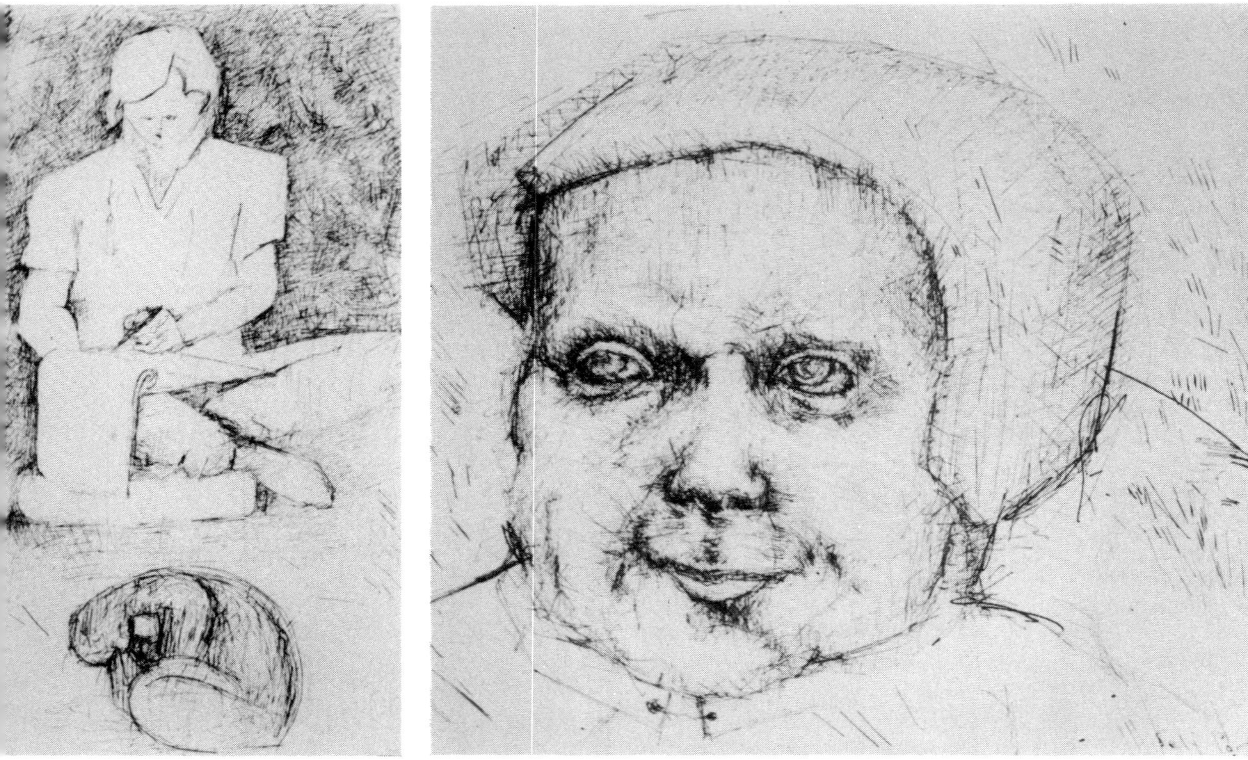

Two of the many drawings done by a 16-year-old and kept in a file/sketch book

It can be used to collect references and to distil aspects of objects and ideas. This form of drawing can be a way of selecting and of rejecting. It can categorise, conceptualise and help focus the perceptions of the drawer. It can be used to clarify subject matter and experiment with ways of presenting the final image.

Drawing as preparation can take two main forms.

The first is the collection of data in the form of ideas, visual references, information about the shape, structure, surface detail, tonal and colour relationships and spatial relationships. Such data may include specific components destined for a painting, a print, ceramics, a textile, and so on. Drawing as preparation may also be non-specific, random and related only to chance opportunities, passing experiences and personal short-term choice. Such drawings become a set of references, available when and if the need arises. Sometimes they are used to mull over later in order to generate an idea for a long term piece of work.

Another function of this type of drawing is as drawing practice. Draughtsmanship, like any other skill, needs to be practised regularly to retain and improve skills, just as the senses used in drawing need to be kept alert. The perceptions are kept alive by such drawing and so is the ability to interpret our responses through drawing. A dancer sets aside time each day to practise steps, learn new ones, grapple with new routines, to keep the limbs supple and the musical responses flowing. Such practice also gives the dancer the opportunity to experiment and push the body a little further toward better performance and interpretation. Artists must also practise their skills in this way and for similar reasons.

The second form of preparatory drawing is where the thinking is specific.

Such preparatory drawing is geared toward a specific end product. The source material and the central idea have been identified. This kind of preparation is concerned with the totality of the image. It is focused on the achievement of maximum ideational and emotional impact in the finished work. It takes the form of trying out different compositional arrangements towards a final selection. An example would be the many drawings made by Henry Moore towards his sculpture of the Northampton 'Mother and Child'. Selection and decision making is at work here.

Both these types of preparatory drawing have been found to be difficult to teach. Young people with the confidence and motivation to use drawing as a thought process in this way are few and far between. Even though many 'O' and 'A' level examinations ask for preparatory drawing as part of the work to be assessed, some teachers are appalled by the cavalier way in which many candidates treat this requirement. This attitude can hardly be attributed to an adolescent conspiracy. Surely it means that the need for and the importance of such preparation is not understood! We must find ways to demonstrate that preparatory drawing leads to better skills, better perceptions, more confidence, more mastery over ideas, more flexibility and better end results, and that it is enjoyable and satisfying. It means that young people must be taught how to organise their drawing in this way.

The sight of an adult engaged in drawing is very rare both in schools and outside them. It is even rare within the confines of art departments. We accept that young children learn by imitation, so if models of adults doing drawing are rare or regarded as the prerogative of the eccentric or gifted it is hardly surprising that adolescents don't regard drawing as normal and useful. When my students and I regularly drew alongside a group of 14-year-olds these children saw this without any prompting, as helpful to them. It demystified the activity. It gave them confidence to see us struggling with the same problems. They felt less in the role of performers, more as if engaged in a companionable, social and serious situation. By observing how we used our drawings the children saw how each individual drawing need not be an end in itself but a means to an end. This was partly achieved by the way in which we structured and designed the sessions as well, so that through the structure of the lessons and by example we felt we had made several important points.

Preparatory drawing in school could mean lengthy projects lasting for as long as a term. Sketch books are obviously one way of collecting preparatory drawings. A useful start to such work is made by providing each child with a sketch or drawing book. 'Sketch' is a worrying word. It often has connotations of roughness and immediacy which isn't always what is wanted.

Gathering information in the drawing book would initially have to be directed. Making visits to local gardens, shopping centres, markets are a common basis for drawing activity. They can make a useful start to keeping a drawing book. Quite specific tasks may have to be given, such as make a drawing of something you find smaller than your hand, something taller than you are, a person you see, any lettering you can find, a plan of a building or an elevation of a building. Even the time to be spent on each drawing may have to be stipulated. Depending on the place visited the class may be divided up to make drawings of certain aspects. The briefs would have to be carefully worked out beforehand and duplicated so that each child has a copy for reference. Time should normally be given for every person to make a drawing of their own choice in addition. Media would depend upon availability, but there should be a choice and colour should be included in the form of coloured pencils, felt-tips or oil pastels. Everyone should have a bag/box/container to hold their drawing tools!

Another starting point could be thematic and done within the art room or the school. Heads, hands, feet, or objects of clothing could provide the theme. Drawings of 'collections' made by the teacher and the children may be used as a theme, but again careful directions as to timing should be given. Quick impressionistic drawing as well as longer more detailed work can be orchestrated by the teacher, with advice as to what to concentrate on in both cases. Even the scale of the actual drawings may be directed. 'Thumb nail' drawings, three or six to a page, half page, full page, whatever is appropriate, may be made. What is obvious to us shouldn't be assumed as obvious to the children. They have to be taught that the habit of drawing on a variety of scales is a good one. After two or three such directed sessions the books can be taken home and used for drawing from self chosen subject matter. It will probably be necessary to provide briefing about the number of drawings, and about scale and type. This will reinforce what has already been learned, while giving an opportunity for more personal choice.

It is important that the teacher makes a point of seeing this work and commenting on it, or alternatively, and depending on the kind of social interchange in the class group, asking students to look at each others' work and comment. In either case a set of criteria must be provided before and after drawing. These criteria would obviously be partially related to subject matter, the past drawing experience of the group and other particular factors. Included should always be a criterion on the information given by the drawing (shape, structure, surface detail, space, tone, colour) and another on the appropriateness of the media used in the drawing as well as the skill in handling and exploring it.

At some point in this process, based on the teacher's judgement, a proposal may be made to use the collections of drawings as material for a considered image or composition. Thus the use of drawing as preparation would move into the second type where thought is channelled toward a specific end product. This can take the form of a larger-scale drawing, a painting, a print, etc, though the use of other media would again depend upon the pupils' past experience and expertise in that medium.

Big decisions have now to be made. Some individuals may be capable of making them independently, others, probably the majority, will need careful direction.

We are often loath to spend a precious art lesson without any practical activity, but reflection and discussion are a necessary part of preparation for art. Time must be found for the children to make a careful appraisal of their own drawings. During earlier stages of the project the preparatory drawings of known artists may have been shown, but here is an ideal time to reintroduce these examples. Constable's water-colour drawings of cloud formations, Leonardo's note books, the teacher's own sketch book – each can make the point that preparatory drawings trap ideas and information, help to work out the individual components of an image, and enable the artist to try out a variety of arrangements of these components for a final composition. These latter examples will help pupils to understand the use of drawing for this type of preparation and convince them of the usefulness of their own sketch book. Thought and planning can be interesting and can save later frustration. Simple squaring up skills can be introduced, once a relevant decision is made, to translate from the very small scale of the chosen idea in the book to the size of the finished image.

Nothing here suggests that this procedure should always be adopted without variation. Individuals vary in many ways and some may arrive at the 'right' idea after only one or two experimental drawings, later on some will evolve their own strategies for preparation and decision making. The advantages of this form of positive training are manifold. The collection of drawings in the book would record tangible thought processes through drawing. It would demostrate art procedures, and actual evidence of one of the uses of drawing. The collection is personal and evidence to its possessor of a period of development in drawing skills, in perception and in ideas. The teacher too has valuable evidence of a pupil's work over a period of time which can have diagnostic and evaluative purposes. It is also to be hoped that this introductory project will create the habit of using a drawing note book.

A teacher told me recently how a group of 16-year-olds were discussing with him their dissatisfaction with their drawing. They felt they were 'getting nowhere', learning nothing. From his store room he brought sets of work done by the group over the previous two years. That there had been a change for the better was obvious by comparing their past and present work. This was the first time these boys had looked at their own work retrospectively. They found the experience heartening and were motivated to go on. What is more, they were unusually lucky to have their earlier work so readily available.

Drawing as designing

Preparatory drawings have a particular relationship with the drawer. They can be said to be introverted, personal, almost private. Drawing as designing relates not only to the drawer but also to function, to media, to costs and to client. Drawing as designing is outward and public. The distinction between design and art has an interesting educational history from its separate identification as a result of the Industrial Revolution. Even more so than in the nineteenth century our contemporary, technological society demands designers of all types. Designers need drawing skills. It is in this direction that drawing can have a function relevant not only in vocational terms but also in illustrating the important social meanings of designing. A society as heavily materially based as our own, can be massively depersonalising. For the adolescent these realisations can be poignant and demoralising.

When faced with a plethora of mass-produced objects which limit and intrude, which create doubtful aspirations as well as bringing some benefits, the act of drawing may well appear to be irrelevant. This is not to claim that mass production is by definition harmful. It is a function of the art teacher to demonstrate the benefits of such a means of production and the part designers have played in the production of such objects. However, the scale and the complexity of our world of objects and images may seem daunting to young people. The relationship between these worlds has to be taught. This was one of the intentions of the Design Education movement started in the 1960s.

Design Education sought to put Art, Craft and Design Education firmly into a contemporary context. Its impetus comes from a belief in the human need to invent and to make, which is intrinsically bound up with a need for aesthetic satisfaction. Such beliefs have more validity now than ever. By teaching design skills it is hoped to aid the development of the social and political skills of questioning rather than merely accept the environment in which we live. Through practice in, and thus understanding of, the design process, the connection between design and the quality of life offered to people of every social strata may be grasped. Through a knowledge of design it is possible to show how to exert control over the environment and effect change through 'informed' argument.

This direct connection between the quality of people's lives and levels of design skill may seem a massive claim, difficult to prove. There is plenty of evidence, easily available, to substantiate it. Thinking of the area around my own home there are two local housing schemes. One, a block of flats, built in the early fifties, lacking privacy, garden and play space, as well as any aesthetic qualities. It is vandalised and dejected. A hundred yards away is a group of 12 terraced houses in an extremely confined space. However, the houses are so arranged to provide maximum privacy, no windows are overlooked, each has a small garden, and walls and roofing are pleasing in colour and texture. Pride and pleasure is taken in the care of these dwellings. There is scope for the inhabitants to create difference and exercise individuality of style in furnishing, decorating and gardening. At some point these houses and the flats were in the form of drawings, drawings as design. The drawings had to take into account certain constraints. The space and the money available would figure largely in the possible solutions. In one case the architect seemed to have gone no further than this, in the other the designer had sought to create the best possible solution for everyone concerned, especially for the real clients, those who were to live in the buildings. This design had evolved through an imaginative process aligned to practical considerations. In an architect's design the interrelationship between drawing, mathematics and engineering is obvious, how else would the building stand up, keep warm and waterproof, hold the plumbing? There are other relationships at work in the design. Psychologists, anthropologists, sociologists, zoologists and historians, as well as writers and artists have helped the architect to understand how space, territory, privacy, family and work relationships affect individual and social health. Concerned and creative architects will take this knowledge into account when empathising and identifying with the users of their buildings.

Architecture is one example of the effect of design, and of the way in which drawing is used to 'show how something is made'. Such drawing takes many forms and goes through many stages. It can 'draw upon' preparatory drawing, but it normally has the following characteristics.

1 The drawing is based on a knowledge of the end product.

2 The drawing will take into account the properties of the materials from which the end product is to be made.

3 The drawing will also take into account the processes by which the end product will be made.

4 The needs of the client or user of the product will be a main consideration.

5 Cost of materials, manufacture and marketing will be considered.

6 Aesthetic, including environmental, considerations will be important in the design.

When introducing drawing as designing to children it is important to show by example how drawing is an important part of the design process and how it functions.

The use of drawing as designing can take place in any context not, of course, confined to that of a Design Education based curriculum. Whatever the context it will have some of the above characteristics and always 1, 2, 3 and 6.

Jewellers, product designers, fashion artists can show children their sketch books, preliminary drawings toward a product, scale drawings with careful

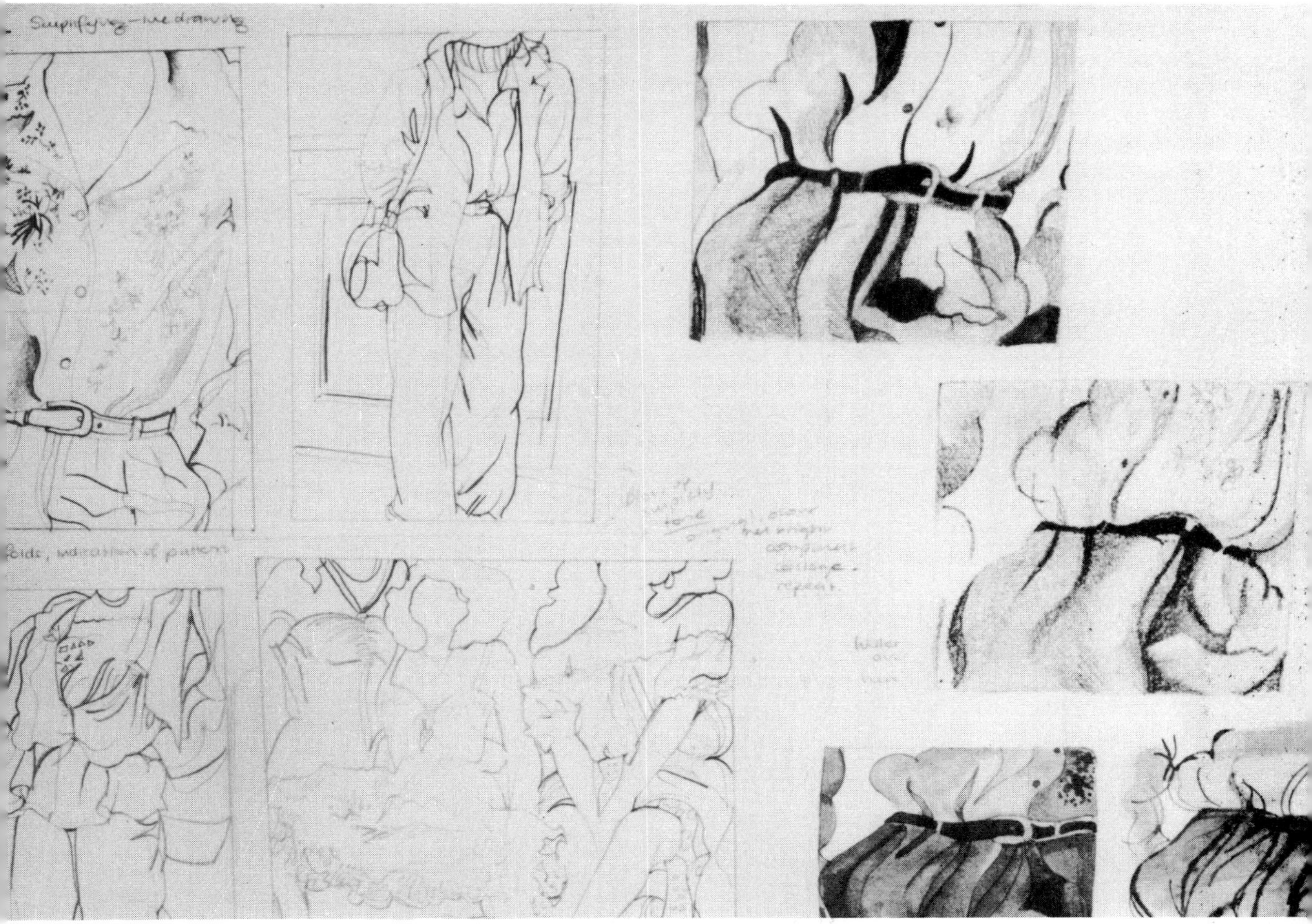

measurements, drawings of details of joins, etc, as well as the end products. Examining these, handling them, and discussion can help the children to understand clearly the need for drawing as part of the design process. Visits to art colleges, industrial, and commercial sites where designing and production take place can be arranged. Carefully organised visits of this kind usually provoke generous responses from the institutions in terms of time and facilities.

Two presentation sheets: sixth formers' different treatments

There is little point in setting drawing projects in design which are purely mock-ups or imitations of design. Too much school work is abstract imitation of the adult world. Practical design products done in school can have real application and can take many forms. These forms must take account of time, group size and local needs.

A group of 15-year-olds designed and made a go-kart for children at a local school for severely physically handicapped children. The idea for the project arose out of discussion about the limitations suffered by the children in the school. The teacher gave case histories and the restrictions on mobility struck home.

The 'designers' drew some rough ideas for the kart before visiting the school as they wished to go there with something tangible to discuss. These first ideas took into account safety factors and their 'clients' physical limita-

Developing a drawing from observation into a design for textiles by preparatory drawings which experiment with different treatments

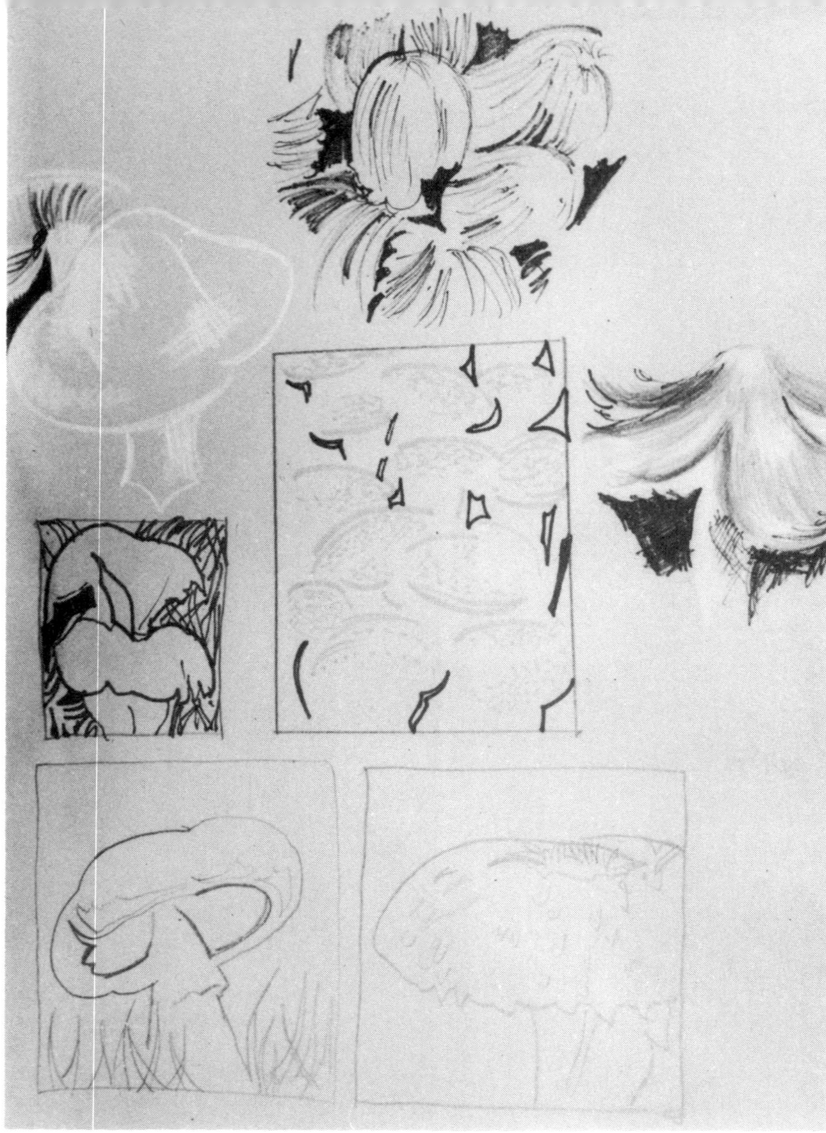

tions as far as possible, from hearsay. A visit was then made to the school and the 'designers' and the 'clients' together discussed the drawings. It was pointed out that the kart must accommodate a wide variety of different sized child. The designers hadn't realised that only a few of the children had enough physical coordination to propel themselves.

The drawings were taken back to school and modified. Some worked individually on an idea, others collectively. A second visit was arranged and the clients chose the design they thought to be the best for the purpose and the most attractive, but suggested incorporating ideas from a number of the designs. Once this decision had been made scale drawings were produced and the kart made. Meanwhile the clients were asked to make designs for the decoration of the kart which was eventually given to the school. The designers made a photographic record of their visits, the go-kart in production and in use.

Designs for fabric printing, for certain ceramics, for murals, for jewellery should all follow the design procedure. A client need not be invented. The designer can also be the client, as can the school or the local community.

Opposite Four treatments of the same subject as part of a design project

Below Drawings for zoetrope strips to create simple animation and establish the principle of animated drawings

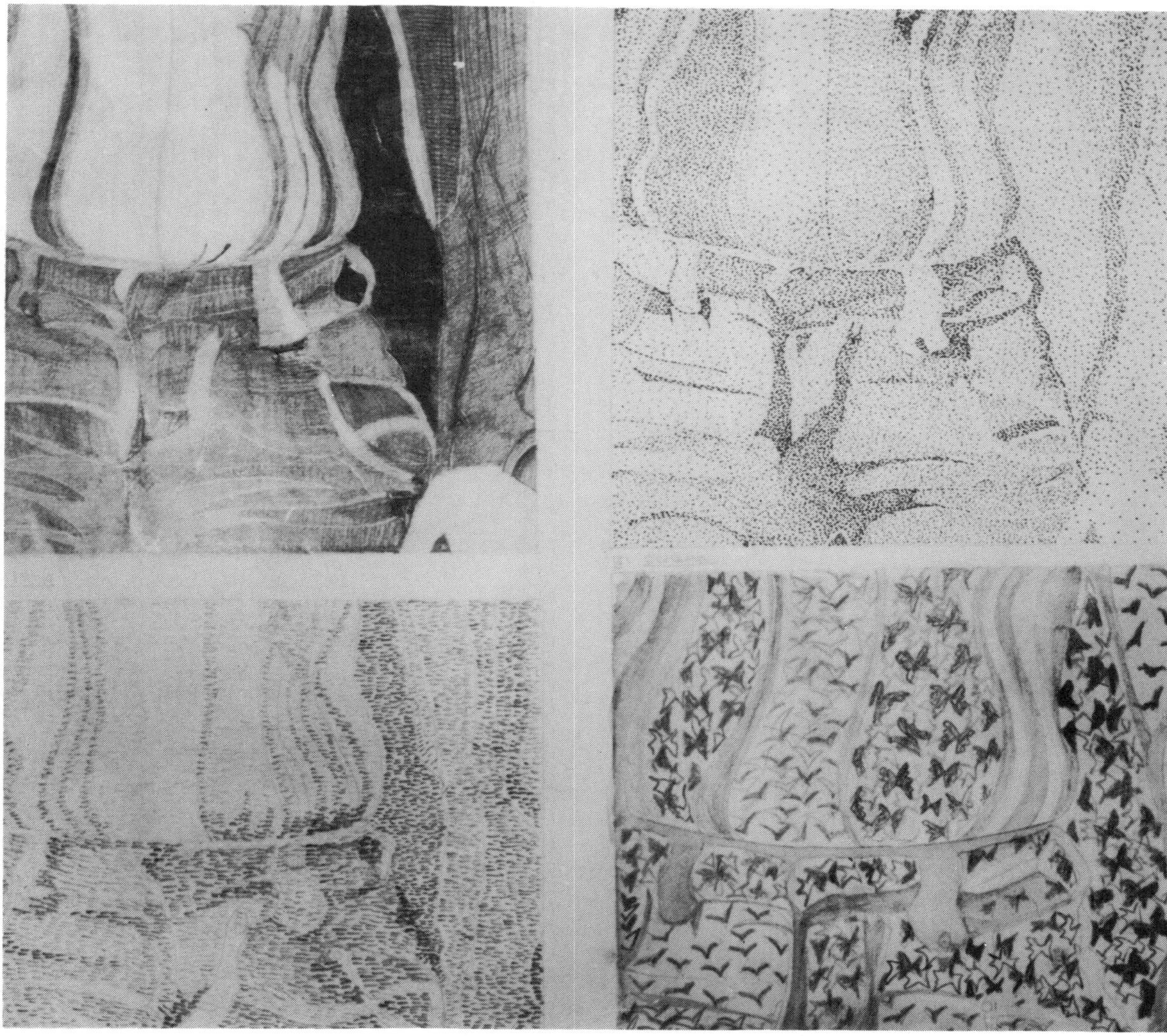

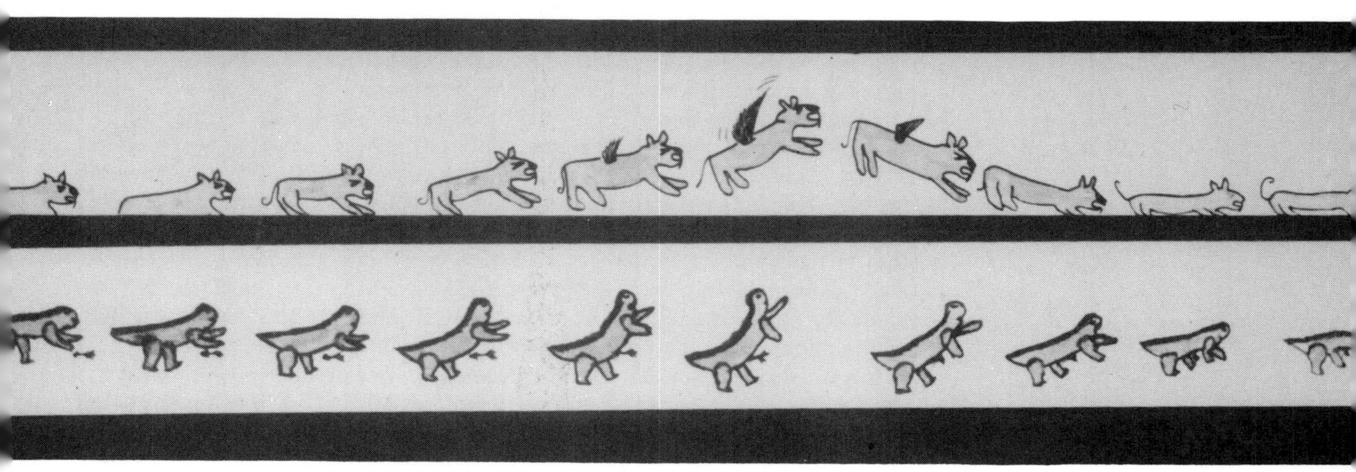

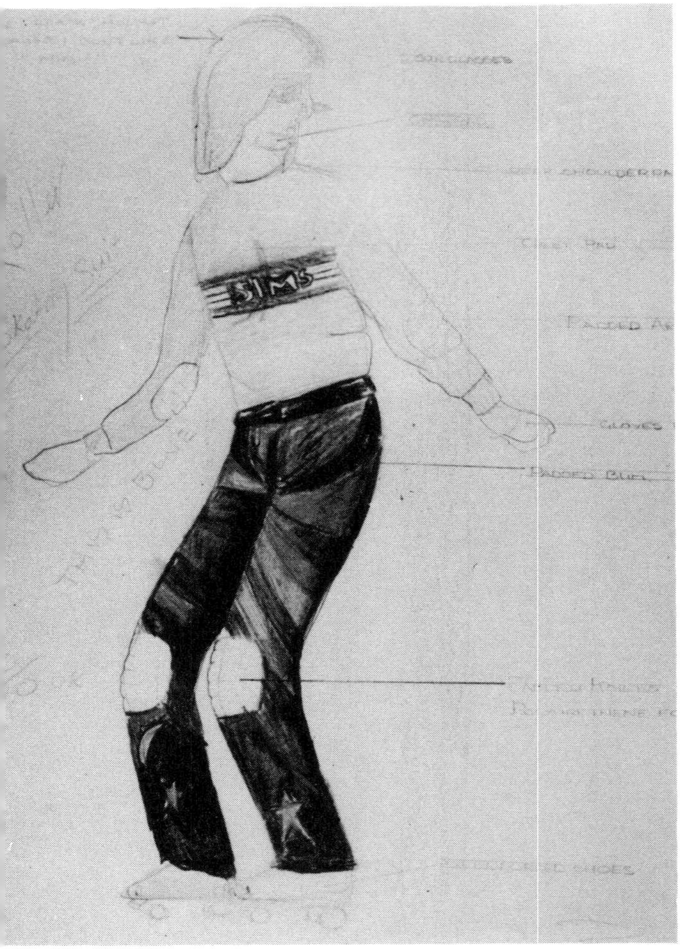

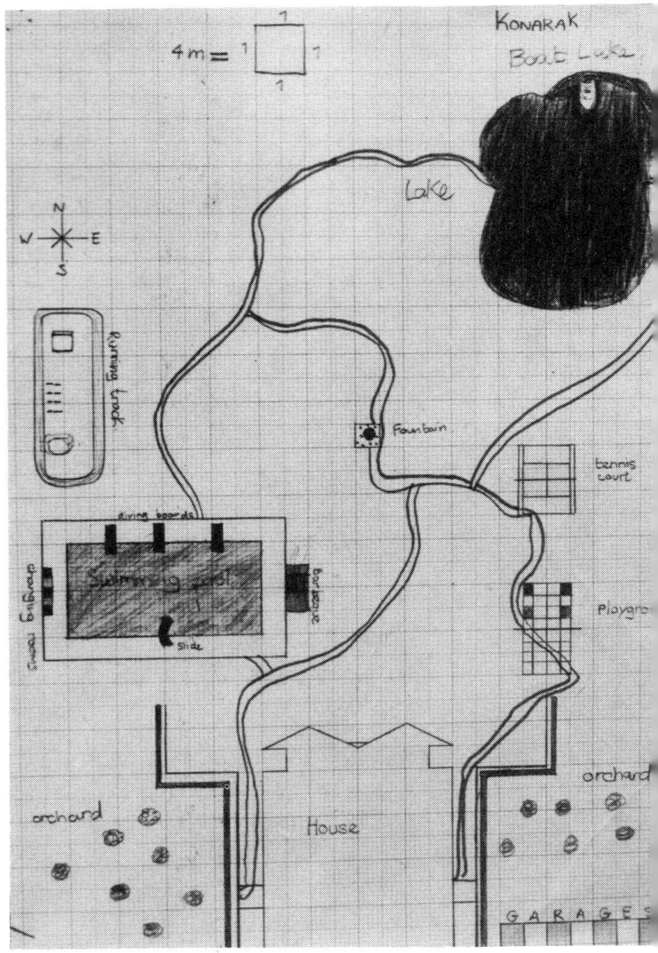

Design for a roller-skating outfit

Right A design for 'My ideal garden'

Drawings for film animation also come into this category. The making of flip books, and zoetrope strips are part of the process of learning the principles of animation. The drawings are also designs for animation. Careful structuring of lessons can result in the production of filmed animations, even with only one camera available. All the criteria of designing are very important in this medium, which offers an activity requiring great discipline as well as opportunities for fantasy, fun and imagination.

Drawing as design can be highly imaginative. Open ended designing is a valuable way of using drawing as a lateral thinking device as De Bono has shown. Young people welcome an opportunity to invent and show amazing facility for it. Their drawings often reveal a remarkable grasp of electronics and physics and are complex, informative and witty. Such drawing can form the start to projects on design and I have seen models made from such drawings. A recent example was a design for a mechanical orange peeler which was made up into a model which showed exactly what the specifications would need to be to make it sturdy enough to be continually usable.

Another group were set the task of making drawings in preparation for the production of a scale model of a swimming pool. The first drawing was based on careful measurements of all the dimensions, plus some drawings of the site and its various features. A vacuum forming process was to be used to make the model and measurements had to be scaled down to a dimension possible on the available press. This required careful computation and the use of various technical drawing devices. From the scaled down measurements a model was made for the vacuum formed mould. The children grasped the principles when demonstrated in this practical way.

It had been decided to use the resulting moulds in an imaginative way and each did a drawing of the pool transformed into the 'pool of their dreams'. The drawings were inventive and original. In the event, instead of a scaled down drawing of the original pool, one of the vacuum formed 'pools' was used as the scenario for a slide and tape 'story' instigated and realised by the children.

These examples of projects show how drawing as designing can function in a variety of ways. It gives adequate opportunity for the free-wheeling imaginative and personal use of drawing aligned to drawing for a specific purpose within given constraints.

Drawing as information

Drawing always informs. For the executant the act of drawing is a charting of information about the content of the image and its relationship to the formal qualities of the style and of the media used.

Examined by a responsive audience it can inform on a factual and feeling level. When I first visited the Tuscan landscape my familiarity with Italian Renaissance art informed my response to it. The familiarity of what I then saw, based on my experience of Della Francesca, Mantegna, Fra Angelico,

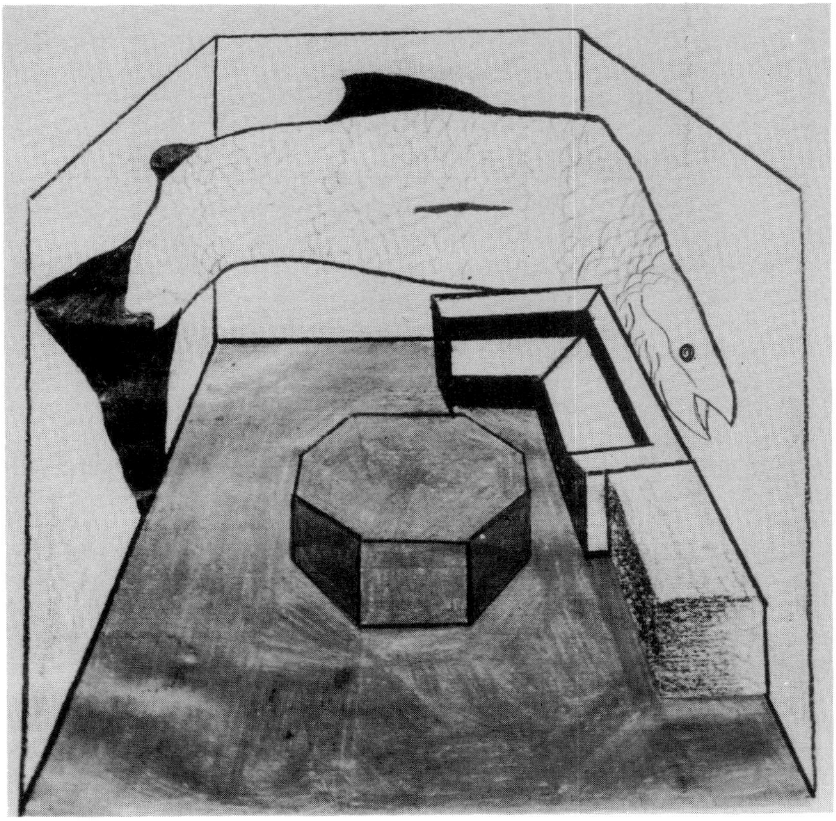

Each child was asked to design the ground plan for 'A room of my dreams' then taught to convert this to an elevation in perspective. Some of the results had a disconcerting perspectival quality, but were both excitingly individual and highly surrealistic

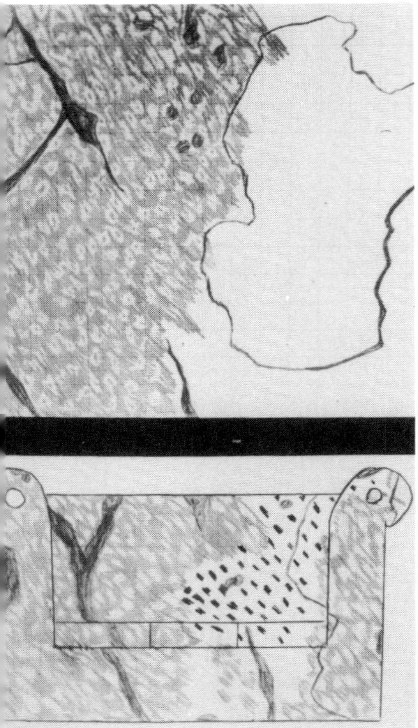

Design project. The children were asked to make a study of particular surfaces and then to think of the drawings they had made from these surfaces as a cover or surface of a functional object such as a sofa or vehicle. This is one design solution

Giotto and others, informed and enhanced my perception. I saw clearly the logic of the Tuscan agricultural methods and of the building styles, my aesthetic response was heightened and I was moved by the evidence of historical continuity and the long, close relationship between human effort and landscape.

The intentions of these Renaissance artists can hardly have been connected directly to my responses to their work centuries later. The way in which the paintings informed me was dependent on accidents of opportunity and my own personality. And yet it is arguable that the works of Giotto, Mantegna and Della Francesca fell clearly into the category of drawing under discussion, at the time of their making. Mantegna's drawing of the Expulsion from the Garden of Eden, Giotto's of the fatal kiss in the Garden of Gethsemane told a familiar story to the people of that time, but the form of their telling conveyed a new message, specific to the new humanism of that time.

There are images whose primary function is to give specific messages. The examples just given were ideologically placed in their own age. That they inform my perceptions after such a long period of time in ways which go beyond their direct ideological content is no doubt due to qualities which supersede their original function, even though they still inform us, in an historical sense, in a way that is as forceful as when they were first made. Our own times produce many images which function in the same way. Political groups well understand the power of imagery to inform, from the logo which provides an easily identifiable symbol of a group, to the poster or cartoon which makes a complex ideological point. The work of individual artists, whether or not they are 'aligned', can perform the same function. Goya's images of war, Picasso's Guernica, and the posters which came from Atelier '68 at the time of the student unrest in Paris inform in a style pertinent to their time and its current peroccupations. Their messages are strong and unequivocal. They demand of the recipient a direct engagement and an acceptance of the visual codes they employ.

Some visual codes are more or less universal. Most of us would respond to → by looking or turning right. Others, such as X are more ambiguous. Our reading of this last symbol would depend on its context. At the bottom of a letter it would mean one thing, painted on a closed door another. Familiarity with the symbol and its context would differ amongst different groups of people. As with the scripts of language, the symbols employed in drawing have to be learned.

There is a vast difference in complexity between drawing with a strong ideological message, such as 'Guernica' or Stanley Spencer's 'The Raising of the Dead' and the directness and simplicity of the Women's Liberation symbol or the CND sign. Both types of image, to be understood, require that a contract be agreed between the informer and the informed, which includes the acceptance of the visual code being employed.

The ability to give and to gain information through drawing is seldom disputed. Psychological research in perception even suggests that we have an innate ability to receive information in this way. The development of this capacity to give and receive information through drawing is a strong argument for the teaching of drawing. Art education in schools has tended to 'back off' from offering young people the opportunity to develop skills in this direction in any specific way. It may be helpful to begin to list examples of informational drawings, that is drawings whose main function is to impart a specific message.

Political posters and cartoons have already been mentioned. Propaganda posters, as in the last war, exhorting the population to refrain from 'careless talk', or to comply with black-out regulations would be another. More contemporary everyday examples would be motorway signs for food, petrol, lavatories and phones, safety signs to warn of the dangers of poisons, of electricity, of inflammable gases and liquids, as well as the availability of first aid, hospitals, police, and breakdown agencies. Other forms of drawings which give useful everyday information would be underground and over-ground rail-maps, street maps and shopping-centre maps. More conplex but equally common drawings which help people in their everyday lives would be A-Z street maps, ordanance survey maps, foot-path maps and gazetteers. Instructional drawings are common in our society. These can range from drawings which tell children how to wash a doll's hair or play a game or assemble model kits, to drawings which inform us how to load cameras, assemble furniture, make garments, use power tools, wire plugs, prune trees, propagate plants, change tyres, drive cars, and use kitchen implements.

Informational drawings which rely upon particular expertise would include contour maps, illustrations for reference books on birds, plants, trees, of antiques and heraldry. Into this category would come mathematical and scientific drawings, technical drawings, architectural drawings, engineering drawings and so on.

The addition of language integral to the drawings would depend upon the function of the drawing and its application as well as the content. Syntactical language could not be universal or international, though naming could some-times be.

Projects on informational drawing in secondary and primary schools can be valuable and enjoyable. They offer situations where the success of the drawing may be tested in practical terms and they can also be pleasurable by being in the form of game playing. As well as demanding a paring down of the ambiguity of the drawing they can develop graphic skills and attention to a central idea. They demonstrate the use of drawing as a direct form of communication and show the need to develop particular forms of drawing, skills not necessarily dependent upon purely representational drawing.

Informational drawings provide comprehensible criteria for assessment since they can be tried out in practice. Many teachers use informational drawing as a teaching method. Charts showing the stages of lino printing is a good example of how informational drawing can be used as a teaching aid. The various tools, cutting method, inking-up and printing processes can be shown graphically and in conjunction with example and demonstration, providing a useful *aide-memoire* to individual children. Such an experience could be a useful example to a class of the use of drawing as information, especially if the teacher feels confident enough to ask the children to com-ment as to the usefulness of the drawn charts.

Such an opportunity to test the efficiency of informational drawings, as recipients, may make a telling introduction to children's own experience of making drawings which give specific information. Children show great inventiveness and enjoy making such drawings. Projects based on this aspect of drawing can take many forms. They can range from drawing alternatives to those in common use such as motorway signs, to ones which would fulfil a local need, for example in the school, to others which can be more fanciful, individual, transient, and fun. Street maps which show how to get from the school to a particular place are often needed, especially in a multi-site school. The making of such a map plus a chart showing other information about the school and its amenities would be an excellent project, better done by a pupil than by a teacher if directed toward new first years. Alternatively one

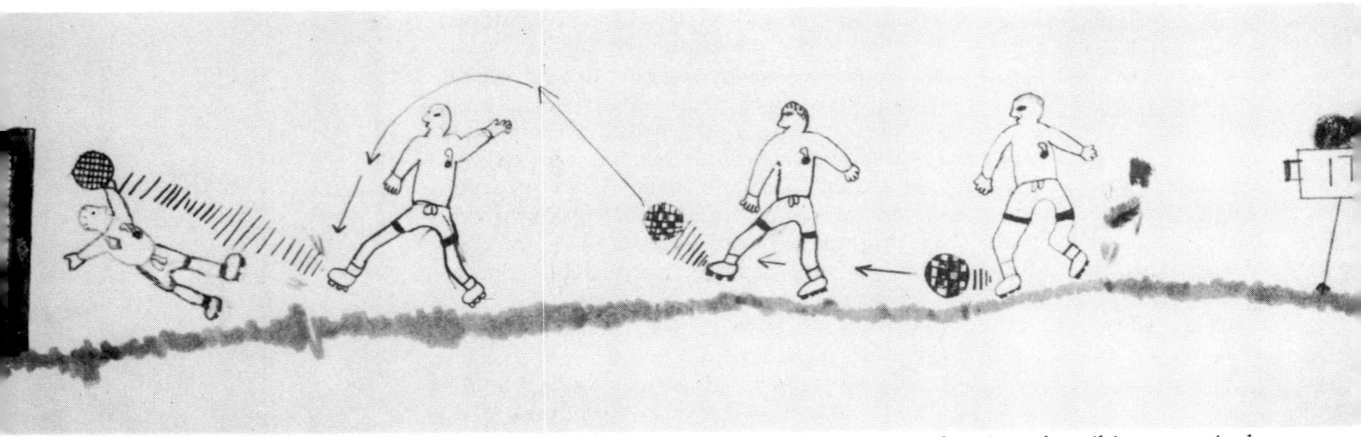

An informational drawing telling us how to make a move in football

group of children could be asked to prepare drawings describing a particular art activity which they have already done. For example a group who have done a photography or animation course could make drawings of processes which would form a visual pack for use by another group of children about to embark on the same process. A cooperative and sympathetic teacher can use the results, report back on her own opinions as to their usefulness, and ask the receiving class to do the same.

These types of project require longterm planning of a kind often difficult in many schools, but they do have great advantages. They are real projects where drawing is being put to a practical use rather than as an imitation of reality. The efficiency of the work can be tested in practice. Such projects demand care in presentation as well as clarity in the ideas, also persistence in carrying through the work is demanded. They can offer an opportunity for a class or group to work collaboratively if various groups undertake parts of a whole information pack. Another advantage is that real-life projects such as these usually demand some kind of reproduction such as photocopying, even screen printing or photography. The adaptations of drawings to these forms of reproduction is another stage in enabling children to understand both the demands made on the graphic designer, and the reason why so many of the drawings they commonly see are in certain forms.

They demonstrate how informational drawings start from a need, that the characteristics of the recipients are known, that they demand certain visual styles where clarity and sequence is important. They show the way in which drawings are modified according to the potential and limitations of forms of reproduction. Through such projects the inter-relationship between an individual's drawing and the mass media may be demonstrated.

Drawing as information can also provide an opportunity to link drawing with other aspects of the curriculum. Collaboration between teachers of history, of modern languages, of design and technology, geography, social science, and so on, and the art teacher could, with careful planning, provide an opportunity for drawing to be seen as important to other activities. Illustrative work for history or environmental studies projects could occasionally be done in art lessons. The teacher of drawing, provided with the information to be conveyed, is ideally placed to advise on styles, suitability of media and aesthetic considerations.

Time-tabling, the demands of the art syllabus in the school and the reluctance of other teachers to collaborate may make long term or linked projects impossible. The personalities of the children, the discrepancies in ability and the social climate in groups can also present difficulties though these are usually easier to overcome. However, short term projects on informational drawing can also elucidate the function of this type of work and its characteristics.

Here game playing can play a part. One of my students recently used a series of ideas for informational drawings such as, 'Make a series of drawings to show a new boy how to get to the headmaster's office from this art room', 'Make a series of drawings to show a person from Mars how to make a cup of tea', 'Make drawings which show a move in football', 'Make a series or one drawing describing a sport you like', 'Draw instructions to show where all the materials and equipment are to be found in this room'. These tasks were typed on cards and presented to the children in the form of a 'lucky dip'. No exchanges were allowed until after the drawings were made. Then each person was asked to award points to the drawing received on a set scale. To avoid as far as possible favouritism, and the reverse, the drawings were anonymous to the receiver and each drawing was given points by two people. Accuracy of information was given ten points, clarity in the drawing five, use of media five and general (aesthetic) quality of the drawing three. Thus weighting was given to the success of the drawing in giving information.

Such devices are not necessarily needed to motivate the children, but they can be one way of helping children to judge the drawing according to function. Much depends on the situation. I remember a few years ago a student teacher was asked to work for one day a week with a group of boys classified as 'school refusers'. The boys were known to have a common interest in motor bikes. The student was a motor bike enthusiast also, and had luckily been given a bike in need of a full overhaul. The boys were keen to do the work and set to work to dismantle the bike with enthusiasm. The random way in

Another informational drawing. A very beautiful description of a vault

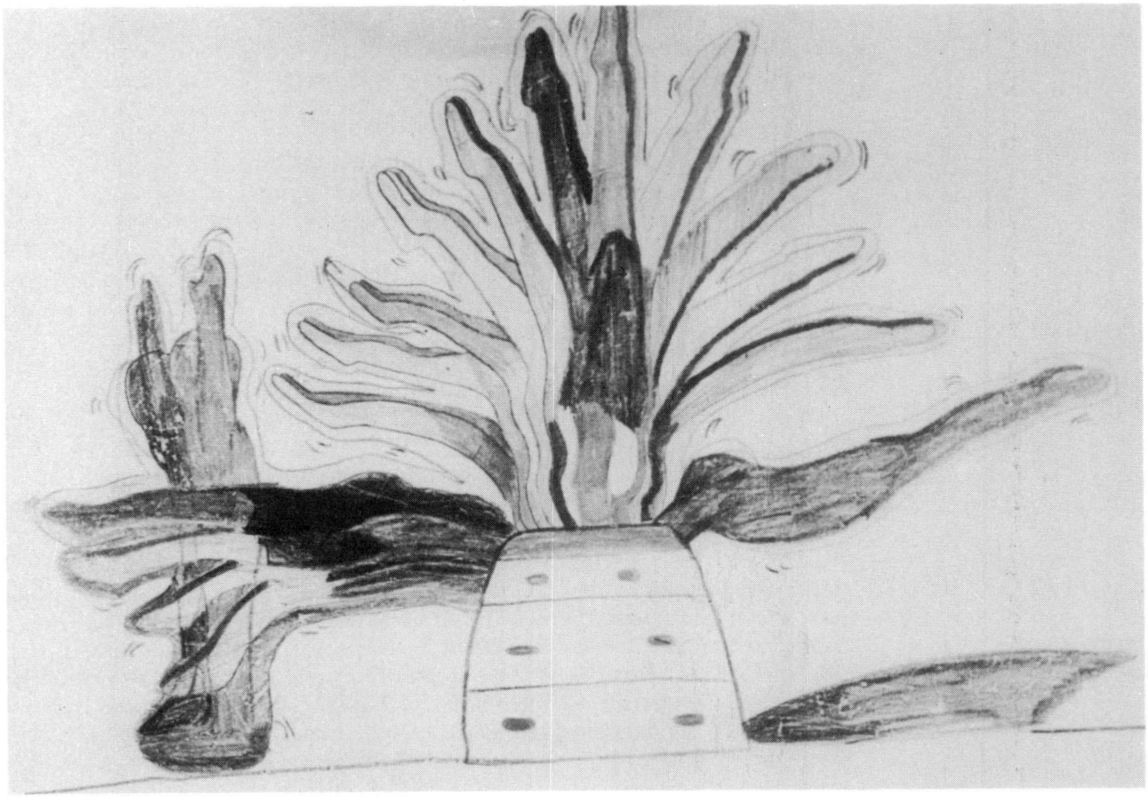

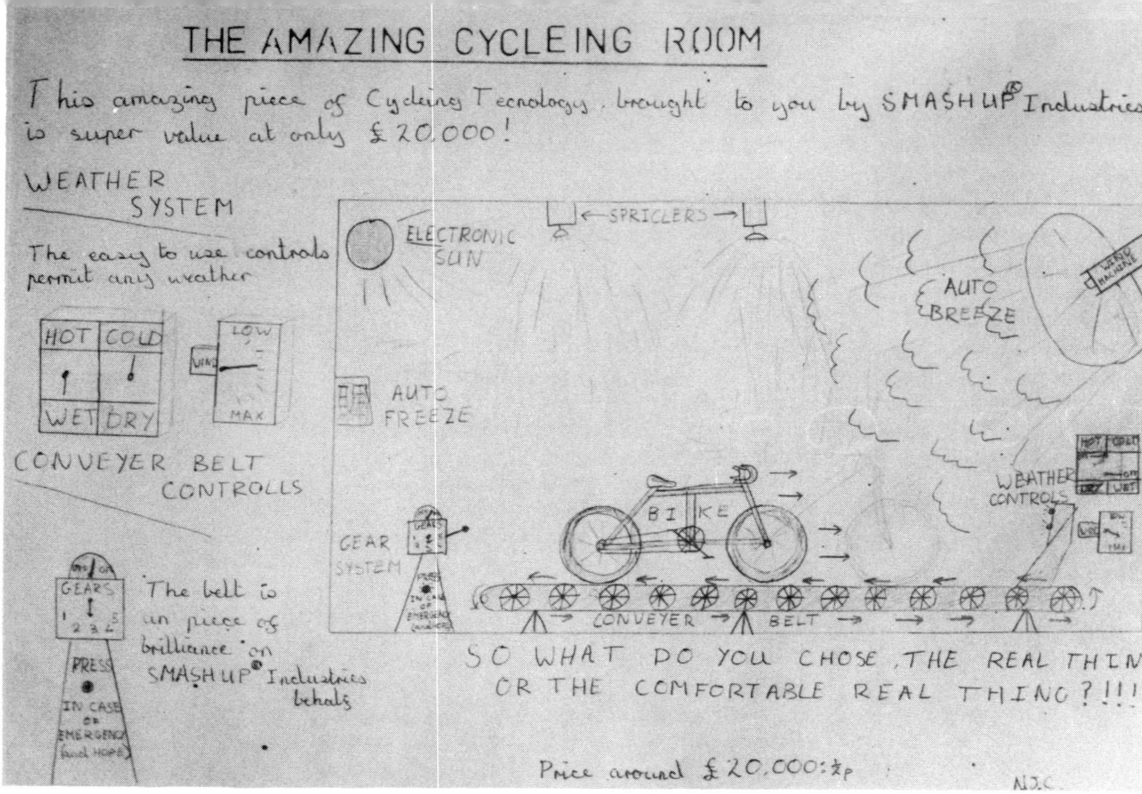

Informational drawing

which they began was pointed out as being hopelessly inefficient since they would have no record of all the parts and their relationship one to another. The boys had another common characteristic, none could read or write with any level of fluency. Drawing was the only way in which the process could be recorded. Thus a log book of drawings was made. This log book improved their drawing skills and had the added bonus of demonstrating to them not only this function of drawing but also that writing is a useful communication skill. Eventually some of them began to use writing as well in the log.

Before, during and after such projects on 'drawing as information', collections of relevant examples of such drawings by the teacher and the children are essential. They can demonstrate a wide variety of style and approach as well as the common use of drawing in this way. Many teachers fear that showing work leads to 'copying'. There is no reason why children shouldn't be imitative in their own drawings. It could be argued that image making, after early childhood, is based on seen images rather than basic sources. Certainly most artists claim the importance to them of the influence of other artists on their work in the formation of a personal style. This would be as true of the graphic as of the 'fine' artists. It seems inevitable that adolescents will derive ideas and styles from others to a certain extent.

All communication systems depend on tradition. Innovation can only work when it has an identifiable connection with traditional forms. The teacher's function in this respect is to help children to confront and to understand as wide a range of drawing styles and systems as possible including that of their peers. Many of the familiar inhibitions of adolescents observed by teachers are due to feelings of inadequacy. This felt inadequacy is not just in the face of the drawing products of the adult world, but also evidence of a fear of exposure to their peer group. The teacher of drawing has an important role in demonstrating publicly the qualities of the drawings of individual pupils to other pupils. Informational drawing provides a perfect vehicle for this where success is not primarily centred on value judgements.

Drawing as a personal statement

We all hold ideas and emotions too threatening and frightening, or too pleasurable and exciting, to keep to ourselves. Drawing is an important answer to the drive to externalise such aspects of our inner world. There are thoughts and feelings we need to examine in order to understand them better. Much art is a manifestation of these urges, largely in the form of paintings or sculpture. Think of Munch's 'Scream', Van Gogh's 'Cornfield', Michel Angelo's 'Slaves' and how they have become part of our iconography. It is surprising that drawing, since it is even more immediate than painting or sculpture, isn't more acknowledged as having this function.

It is important to distinguish between this form of drawing and drawing used in therapeutic way. Therapeutic art has a particular para-medical use. It takes place in a professional situation set up as a healing device or as a method of diagnosis, usually for the benefit of psychiatrists and their patients, and as such it is not the province of the teacher of drawing. However one of the valid and universal functions of drawing is ameliorative, even cathartic. Fears, obsessions, pleasures, desires, preoccupations, thoughts and ideas are

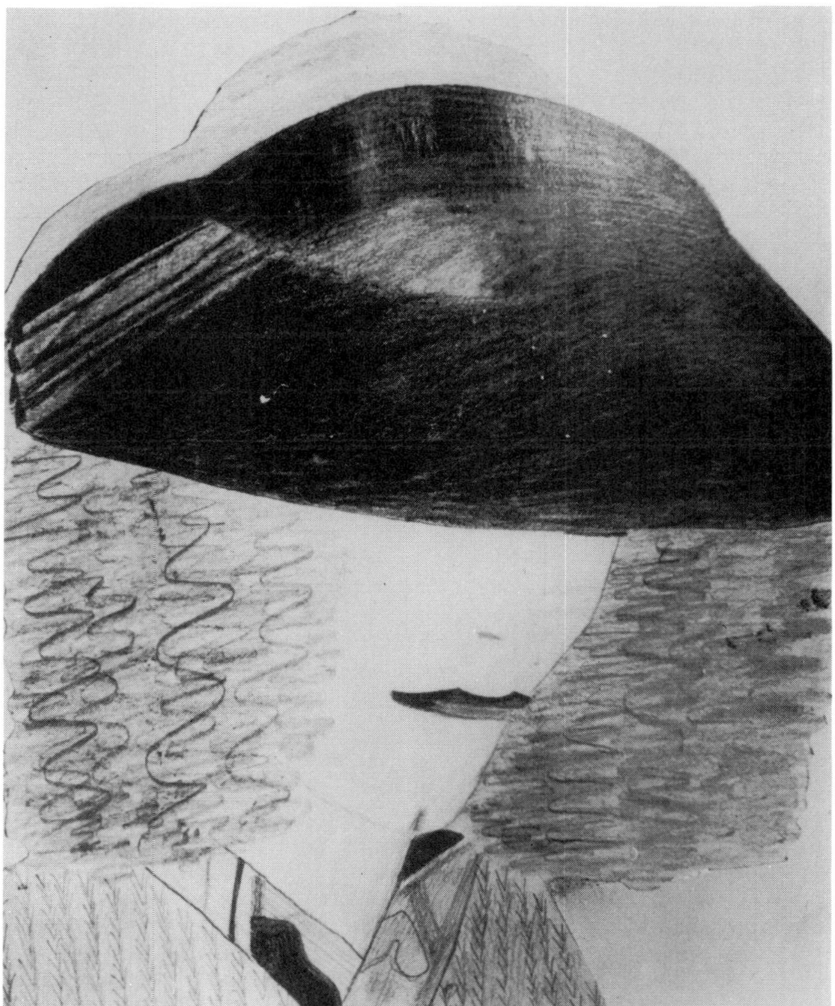

Personal image derived from a photograph, made by a 14-year-old

integral to the human condition and seek an outlet of expression and communication. This function of drawing figured largely in the 'self expressive' school of art education. Marion Richardson, whose name is usually associated with this movement, believed that a rich store of imagery is locked in all of us and that the function of the art teacher is to provide the key to unlock this store and enable the child to release those images which derive from the personal perceptions of each individual. Herbert Read further developed her theories. In *Education Through Art* he propounded his belief in the individual artistry of every child and in the importance of valuing their imagery in the context of that child's personality. The self-expressive school of art has been profoundly influential on art education attitudes and practice. A respect for individuality has been the great bonus of this, but an over emphasis on this function of drawing to the exclusion of others, with its concommitant fear of teacher intrusion as an impediment to individuality has been quite damaging. On the contrary the teacher has a positive role to play in the teaching of this as of all the other functions of drawing.

In order to externalise thoughts and feelings, there must be the means to do so. What are these means in drawing? They would include a knowledge of the expressive qualities of all the media of drawing through example and experience and the confidence to attack such drawings. How would such confidence be acquired or fostered?

'The dilemma of adolescence is its selfconscious and self-critical nature. Drawing as a spontaneous activity tends to fall away, originality is hard to achieve as adolescents tend to be imitative. They seek for models.' This was how a group of teachers expressed what they felt to be the main difficulties in teaching drawing to adolescents. This question of 'models' is a crucial one. It is better to acknowledge the need for them and have some control over providing some of the right quality and variety rather than, through a fear of mechanical copying, fail to have any control over this important aspect of drawing education. All artists and designers have divined much about their craft by studying, and even plagiarising, the styles and subject matter of others. Providing models is not enough, ways to benefit from them need to be taught. Other art forms such as film or writing which also make personal responses to events can help validate this particular function of drawing.

The use of 'models' or examples of drawing is often criticised as providing secondhand experience. Direct experience as a stimulus for drawing is an essential. The best function of examples of drawings is to enable the drawing response to firsthand experience by giving direction as to interpretation. Personal response to experience can be inhibited where there is a fear of censorship and moral judgement. Creating a working climate where drawings in the form of personal statements are made and taken seriously is not always easy. Many adolescents make drawings which challenge the values of the teacher. They may be crudely racist or sexist and so violent that the teacher finds them difficult to deal with on any level of objectivity. Such images can't be merely tolerated. They have to be both acknowledged and challenged. Too often such phenomena are either banned (and so go underground) or looked at without demur (and thus accommodated as acceptable).

The pressures of the peer group and the pervasiveness of the mass media have to be acknowledged in this as in other uses of drawing. The imagery of both will inevitably appear: both can provide models. Are drawings from the media made available in schools often enough to illustrate both the range of drawing styles and the quality to be found in comics, TV and advertising or when discussing the history of drawing? By comparing foreshortening as used in the original drawings of Batman with Mantegna's foreshortened Christ or a Baroque ceiling many points can be made, not least in acknowledging the cultural importance of our times and its relationship with the past. A characteristic of the media is its finish and glossiness. Attempts to achieve these qualities through the use of photography, dry mounting or silk screening can often help adolescents to identify their own work and place it in their 'real' world.

Confidence can be fostered by these provisions. It must also be based on competence – competence to handle materials as well as ideas. This suggests personal control; in the case of drawing competence is control over what?

Teacher: That's lovely Sandra, really good!.
Sandra: But Miss, she looks as though she's falling off her chair, the hands are all wrong and the tea pot's nearly as big as her!

Powerful personal images made by an adolescent

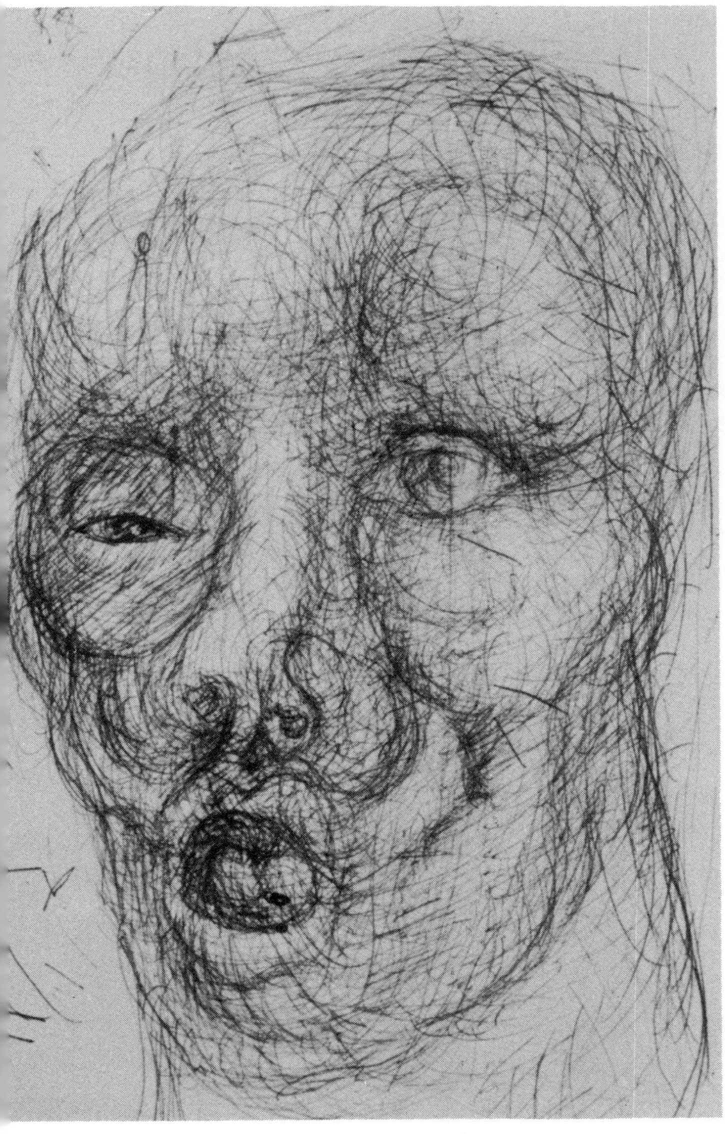

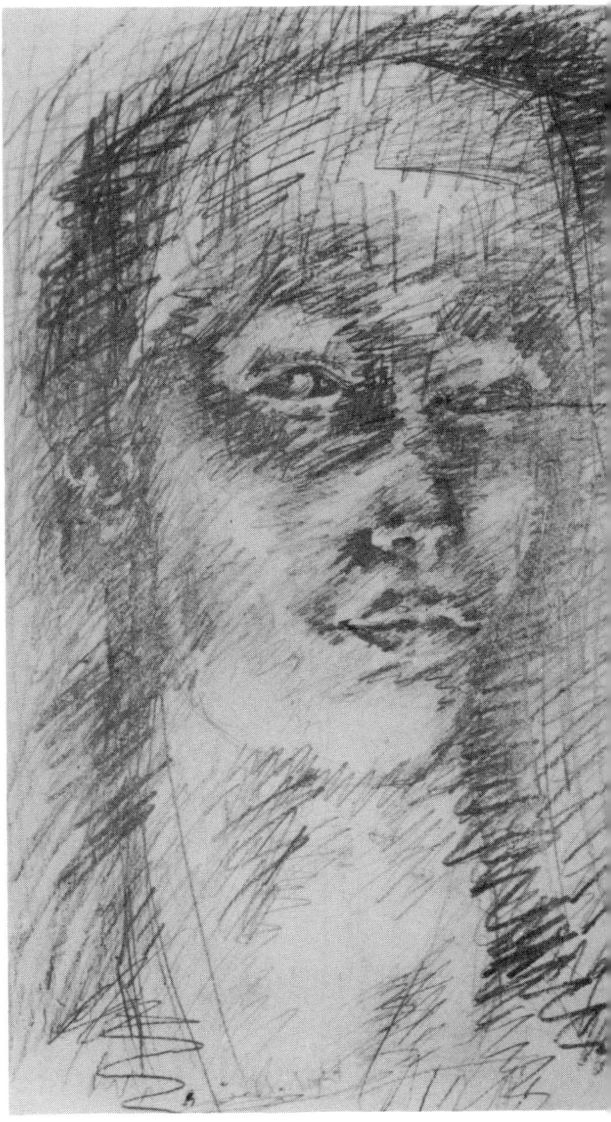

3 The skills of drawing

I experience dissatisfaction with my own drawing on two levels: one is in the realm of idea, where the concept behind the drawing seems ill-judged, incompletely formed or perhaps too derivative; the other arises from frustration that my skill is not sufficient to express the idea graphically.

Ideas for drawing arise as a response to the eventual function of the drawing, from an experience, from a personal interest and as a result of rigour of thought and sincerity of feeling. Without these qualities no matter how skillfully executed, the drawing is likely to be banal, superficial, sentimental, trite or formulaic.

Conversely, without a measure of graphic skill a strong image is unlikely to emerge. Some skill must be present to realise the idea. As a non-dancer I can visualise a dance in my head, I can try to dance it, but without the balance, muscular control and stamina of a dancer I cannot fully realise the dance. Not only will my idea become debased and ludicrous but, increasingly unformulated to myself, it will peter out, starved of a sufficiently diverse repertoire of movements, and sufficient control over those movements, to sustain the feeling and logic of the idea. Similarly, when there is a lack of ability to communicate the visual forms, the impulse and idea for a drawing cannot be realised, in fact very often they cannot even be retained in the mind. Graphic skills are concerned with the mastery of the means toward satisfactorily drawn images. Through these skills form is given to the content of the drawing, which satisfies the impulse of the drawer, and provides an adequate communication of that content to others.

But what are these graphic skills? How are they to be mastered? These questions are what adolescents are asking to be taught. When they say, as they so often do, 'How can I make it look real?'. Doesn't this mean 'What skills do I need to acquire in order to realise my ideas into a drawing, and how do I acquire them?'?

To teach such skills they must first be identified. Like all skills they cannot exist in isolation, indeed it is the exercising of all these skills concurrently that results in drawing. The interrelationship between the skills of drawing is of paramount importance in the act of drawing and again has to be taught. These reliances and relationships can only begin to be understood if those skills can be isolated conceptually. While they cannot be practised in total isolation, teachers can offer situations where the development of one of the skills is the major focus of attention.

A skill which affects all aspects and stages of drawing is what I will call the *perceptual* skill: by this I mean the ability to direct and devote attention and allow the senses to be fully engaged in the act of drawing. *Language* skills are important, for without the correct terminology crude generalisations can seldom be developed into more differentiated and discriminating decisions. The knowledge of the tools and the materials of drawing through practical exploration of their properties and potential are the *craft* skills of drawing. Understanding of the concepts of line, tone and colour and the ability to create a range of these are the *formal* skills of drawing. Finally

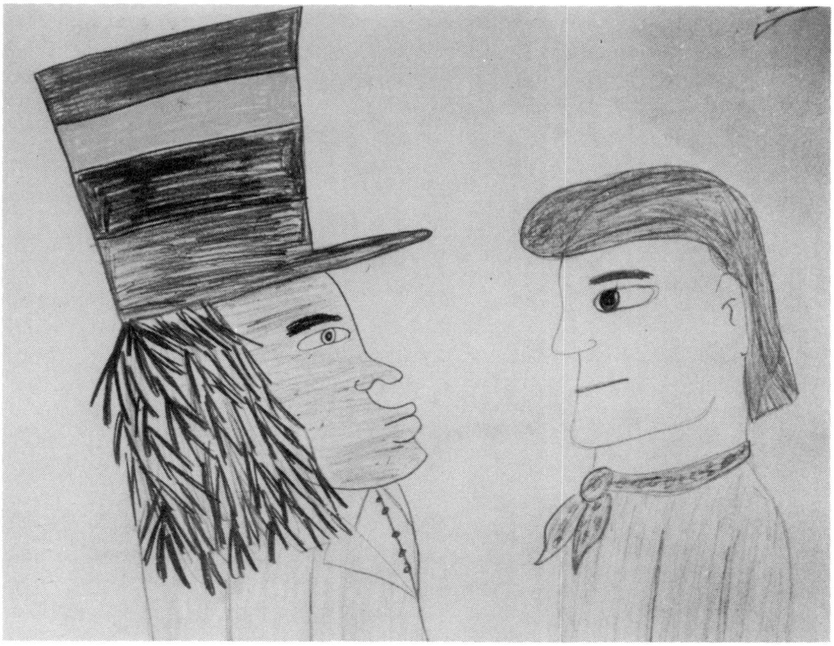

Racial stereotypes in an adolescent drawing

there is the exercise of all the former skills in order to depict volume, space, movement, surface, light, atmosphere, mood, sensations. This is what I will call the *coding* skill of drawing.

The perceptual skills

Earlier in the section 'Drawing as Seeing' I argued that, in the act of drawing, all the senses are engaged, not just the visual. Theorists in perception, looking at the evidence of children's drawing, have suggested that young children naturally perceive the world through all the senses but that there is a shift to more reliance on the visual as puberty is reached, although for a minority of people that would not be so. These observations have led to the theory of visual and haptic perception, which is documented principally in the work of the art educationalist Victor Lowenfeld. There are also helpful sections in this topic in Herbert Read's *Education Through Art*. Most recently Maurice Barratt, in his book *Art Education: a Strategy for Course Development* explains very clearly the distinction between the two in his section on 'Stages of Development'. Briefly the theory is that there is a continuum of perceptual response. At one end of the continuum is purely visual perception. Here the sight dominates all other senses. The perceptions are objective and dispassionate, they take an observer's point of view. At the other end of the continuum there is purely haptic perception. Here touch, taste, hearing and the kinaesthetic senses dominate almost to the exclusion of sight. This type of perception is subjective, participatory and centred on the self. The purely haptic is rare, as is the purely visual, most people's perceptions fall somewhere along this continuum, but it has been claimed that at adolescence about 40 per cent are likely to be predominantly haptic. The way in which people represent the world in drawing is dominated by their perceptual style. Thus the drawing of a strongly visual person is likely to be objective and dispassionate, that of a strongly haptic person subjective, etc.

Sensitive and caring art teaching should aim to cater for these two types,

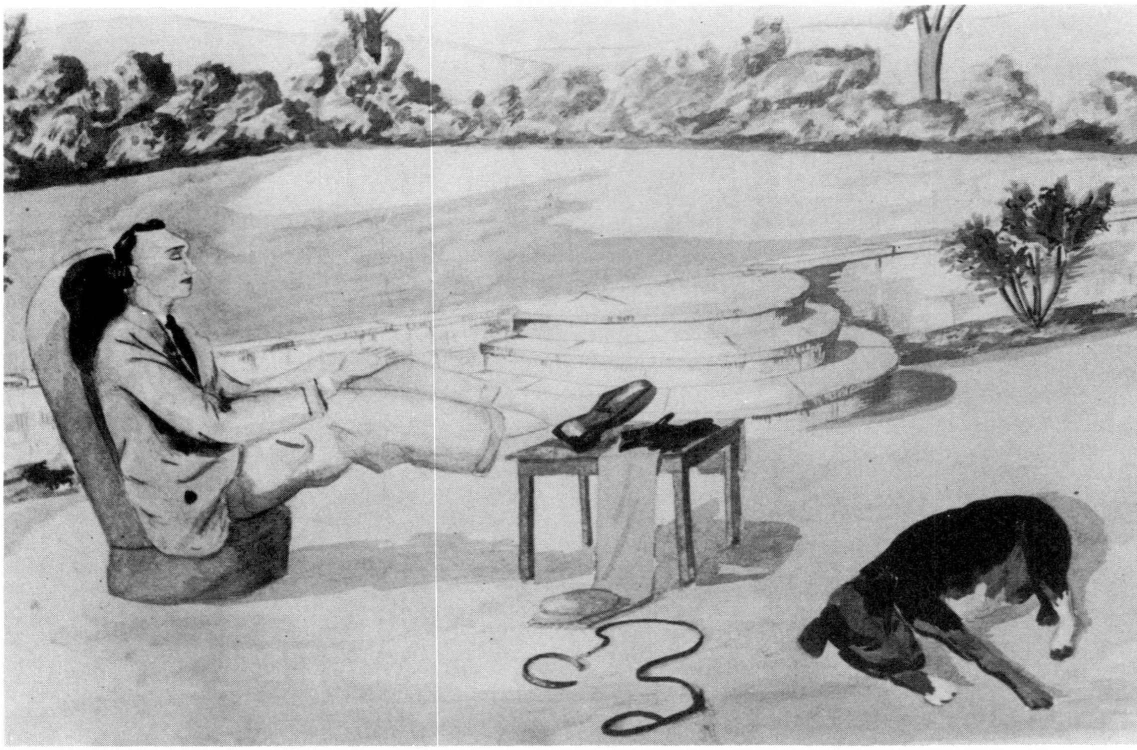

This adolescent drawing of my own is an interesting find. The scene bears very little resemblance to the actual circumstances of my adolescent life. In looking at it I can recall my preoccupation with perspective and shadows

but there are problems. My own observations and a few small studies by students indicate that haptic adolescent drawings are not always easy to identify. There are some clear instances but not many. Many of the drawings studied when seen in isolation seemed to be obviously haptic. When looked at alongside drawings produced by the rest of the class group however, all seemed very similar. Was this due to the nature of the tasks set or to common difficulties with the media made available?

This is not to say that haptic work is characterised by ineptness with materials, rather that our analytical skills are not yet refined enough. The work of children from 14 onwards as seen in schools tends to be produced by children who have opted for, or been chosen, to take an art course leading to a public examination. In my opinion these children, and thus their drawings are likely to be the more visually oriented. They will have been guided and chosen by teachers more likely to be visual types and who know that such work is most likely to be successful in external examinations.

That visual and haptic work is present in adolescent drawing is irrefutable. What is more my observation suggests that visual and haptic imagery can be, and often is, present within the work of any one child. Much seems to depend on the type of task set and to the fluctuating perception within any one personality according to mood or circumstances. Such flexibility and fluidity could be encouraged through the teaching of drawing.

This can be achieved in two ways, through practical projects and through the types of visual references used by the teacher. In practical terms we can construct drawing situations where both types of response are equally viable; we can also offer teaching situations where there is an encouragement to perceive in one way rather than the other. Familiarity with, as well as the examination and evaluation of images of both types is an important part

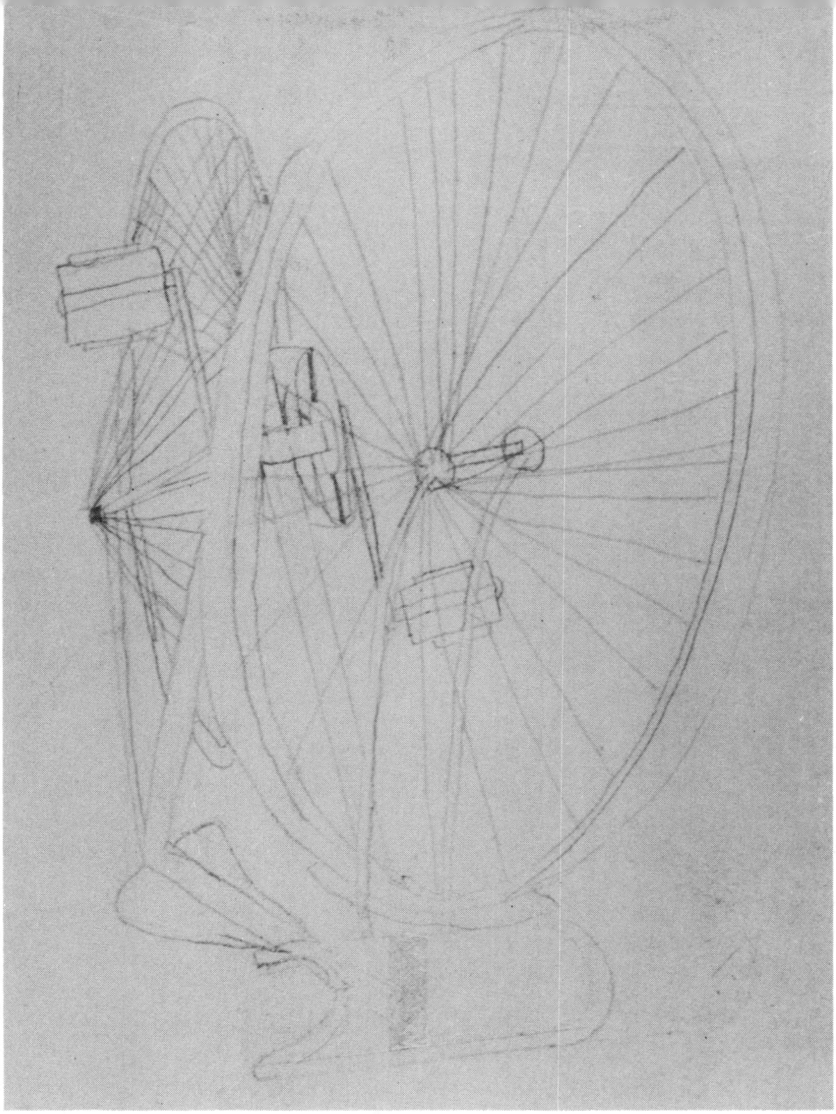

Analytical, 'visual' drawing of a cycle

of the teaching of drawing, whether the images be those of established individual artists, or those of cultures where haptic imagery may predominate, or of fellow artists in the teaching group.

Perhaps it is in one particular traditional aspect of teaching drawing that the difference between the two types is most apparent. So-called objective drawing is a common activity in secondary schools, and an examination subject at 'O' and 'A' levels. Art teachers' attitudes to it vary a great deal. Some think of it as the one tangible aspect of the drawing curriculum where there is a definite place for the transmission of skills; others regard it as the scourge of art teaching, as they see children failing and floundering. But what is meant by objective drawing? The drawing of still life groups, life drawing, plant drawing are all regarded as objective drawing. The common factor in these activities is that the drawing derives from a tangible, given experience, observed. The landscape or townscape, the figure in the chair before us, the collection of objects on the table are present there to see.

An objective response to these events may be impossible because they have accrued subjective meanings for each personality. The person drawn may be a friend or enemy, the objects boring or interesting, or memories and associations stirred. Our feeling response will vary and affect the image

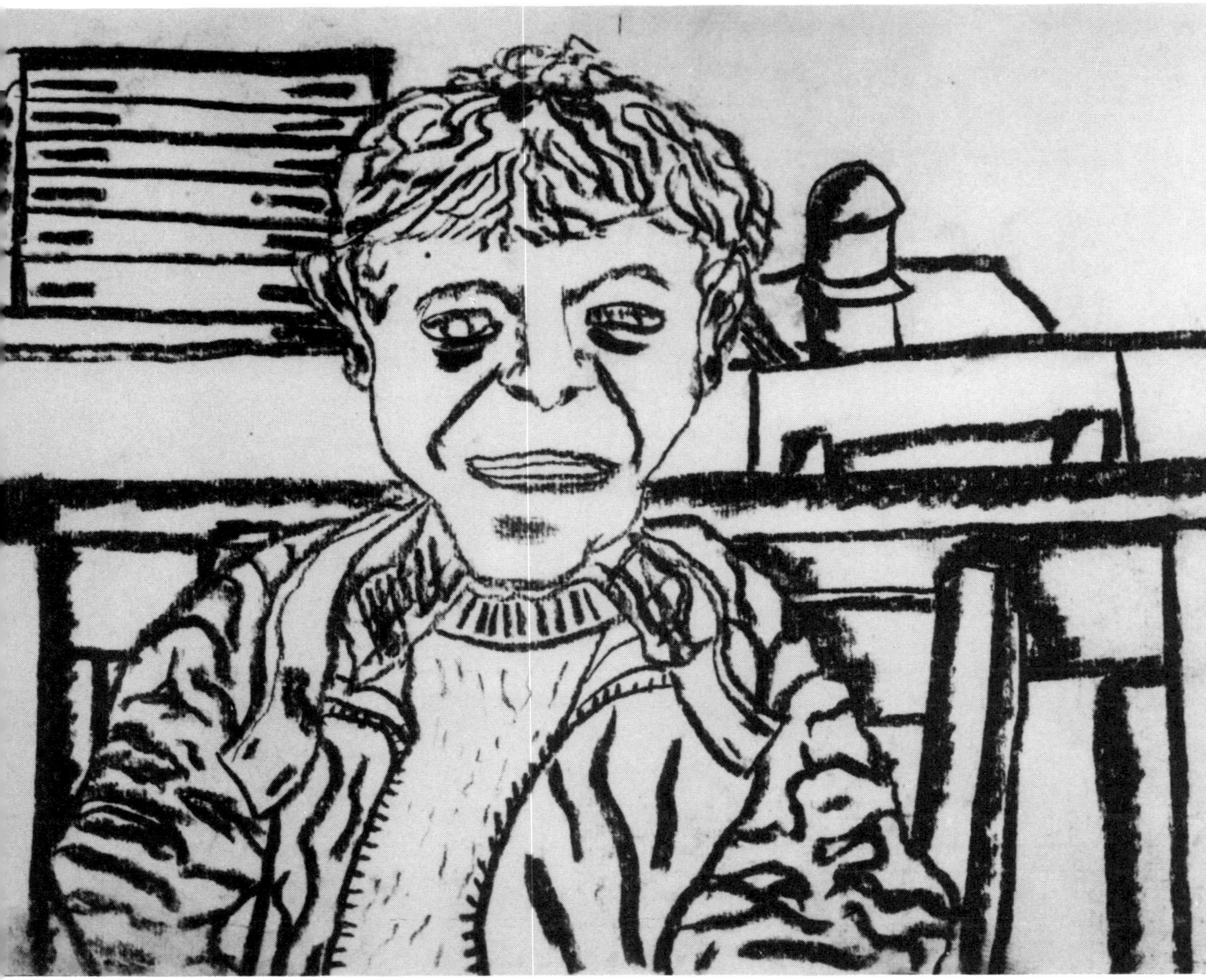

Above and facing Three life drawings from observation by 15-year-olds

A vigorous, strongly linear drawing. The figure and the surroundings are undifferentiated in treatment. Level of observation is high. There is a great deal of information given in the drawing and the image is confident and intense . . . an objective *and* subjective drawing

we draw. Objective drawing suggests we obliterate these feelings, indeed it means that the drawing should be an analysis of the formal qualities of what is before us irrespective of other meanings. Such aesthetic motivation may be possible for the more established artist, but even such a person would have to make a conscious decision to perceive and to work in this way. This is where motivation and perception in the teaching of drawing seem inseparable.

Perhaps we should distinguish observational drawing from objective drawing. Both require the perceptual skill of attention and persistence in attention. Both require the engagement of the senses. The visual person may rely excessively on sight. This is not to say that perception for even a highly visual person cannot be improved by attention to touch, by handling the objects to be drawn or by the kinaesthetic experience of moving round and through what is to be drawn, preparing for a life drawing by taking up the position of the model oneself, thus experiencing the body in that space, the strains of the position, the distribution of weight, the holding of objects and so on. Similarly the haptic person will be helped by the opportunity to develop perceptual skills which rely on sight, on the measurement of pro-

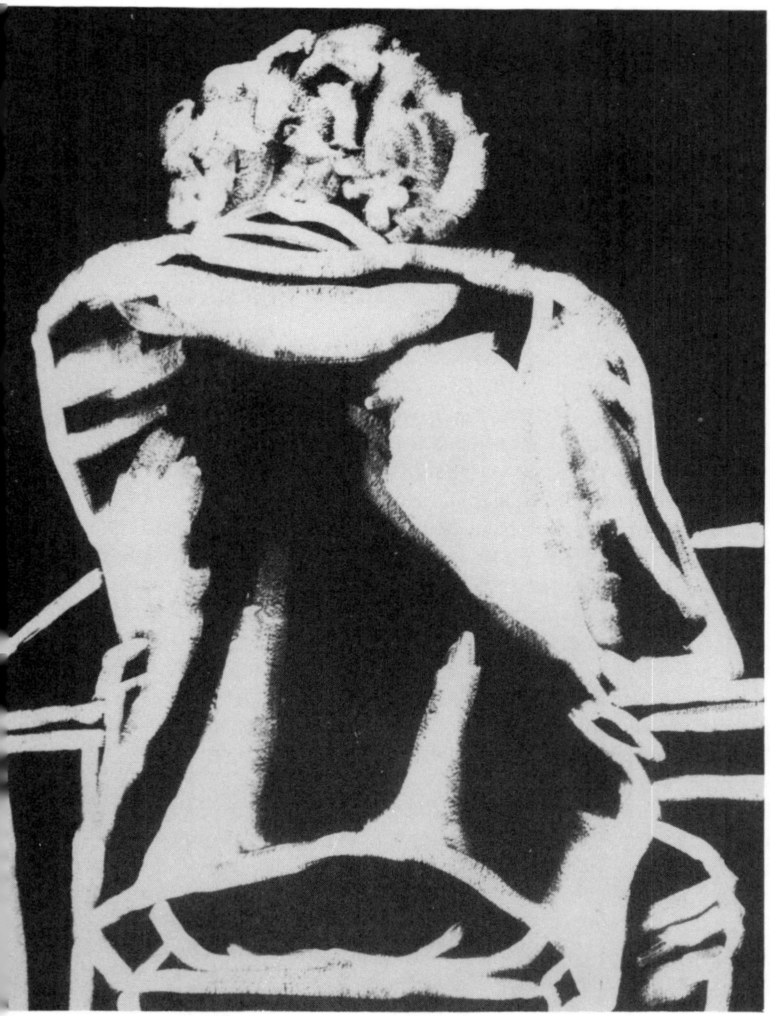

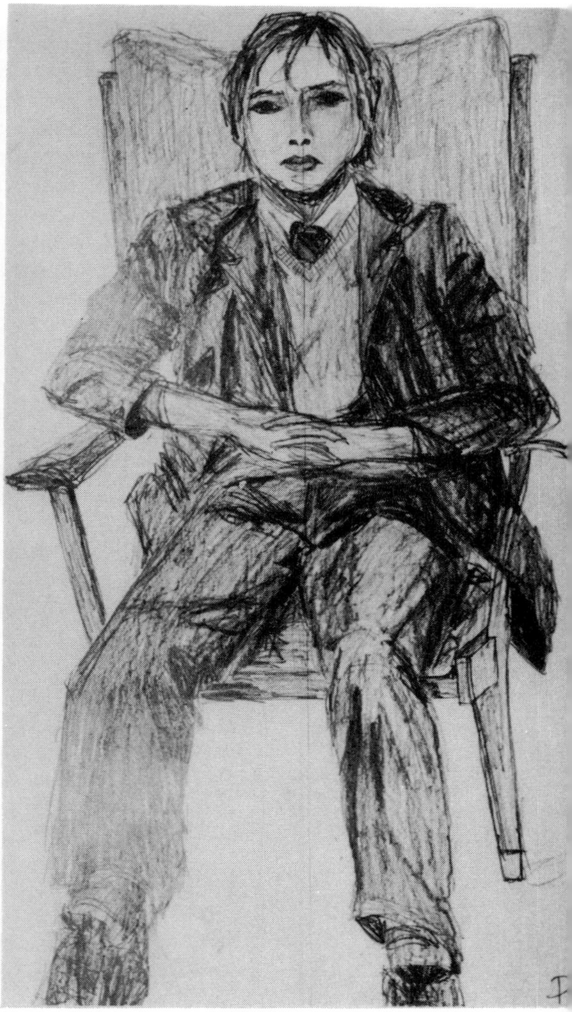

portions and on making discriminating visual analysis of tonality or colour.

We are all afraid of intruding into what we regard as the natural responses of our pupils. Drawing seems such an important vehicle of individuality that we may hold back from any practice which may suggest conformity of response or product. Drawing tasks which are designed to train perceptual skills often seem dangerous in this respect. If, in presenting such tasks, the purpose of the work and the reasons for the presentation or methodology is made clear to all the participants there should be no misunderstanding. There is little point in telling pupils that they fall into two perceptual categories, obviously, but it is possible to demonstrate how drawing can sometimes rely on the ability to make visual analyses and at others on a more kinaesthetic response. We can show how the perceptual skills we use in making drawings and in reacting to them will vary according to the function of the drawing as well as to the personal style of the artist. Such teaching should encourage flexibility rather than conformity.

We seldom hear the term 'subjective drawing', though I suspect that this is often what is meant by 'imaginative drawing', and certainly by 'self expression'. Imagination and subjectivity can be brought to bear while engaged

Left An amazingly realised drawing which I would describe as haptic, but are the impact and the approach objective or subjective?

Above
Note the vertical centre line. The approach is strongly objective. The seemingly confident linear treatment covers a lot of inconsistencies and weaknesses. Even so the personal gesture of the line drawing of the face imbue the drawing with a subjective overtone

in drawing from observation. Analytical drawing can take place in the absence of the situations or objects to be analysed, but not without any perceptual experience of the event. Feelings and associations affect perceptions. Whatever the function of the drawing both objective and subjective approaches can be working on the outcome, for the quality of perceptual skills employed in the drawing will affect its success in fulfilling its function.

Drawing as preparation, as design, as information and as personal statement can all occur with or without the objective content of the drawing being physically present and directly observed. When they are absent how are the perceptual skills exercised? In two ways, through past observed experience, ie memory, and through perceptual sensitivity to the drawing as it emerges, ie aesthetic acumen.

Memory may be present in a tangible form, for example past observational drawings. Memory can be evoked in the act of drawing. To draw an object in its absence can be to recreate its formal and other properties. Memory drawing was a great vogue at the turn of the century. Richard Ablett's 'snap-shot' drawings are perhaps the most popular example. He believed in the importance of training the visual memory. Such teaching is fairly rare now, perhaps because with the media explosion visual references are so commonly available. But is not the ability to conjure up shapes, proportions and spatial relationships in the mind's eye and to convert these images into drawing different from the ability to adapt from photographic and other references? In the sixties there was a great deal of interest in eidetic imagery, which is the ability to superimpose a remembered image of great complexity and detail in front of or between the present world of objects and ourselves. Young children are meant to have this capacity and some remarkable cases have been recorded of older children and adults who have retained it.

Can it or anything like it be trained?

The training of archaeologists, naturalists and detectives shows that specialised perceptual memory can be developed. Why should it not be done in the teaching of drawing? A teacher gave a group of children objects to be looked at handled and examined in as many ways as possible. They were encouraged to consider the shape, feel the surface, weigh the object in the hand, smell it and so on. They knew that they would be asked to draw the object later on. In many of the drawings as much information as they would have normally given in a drawing from observation was apparent in the memory drawing. For others the accuracy of shape and proportion, and the amount of detail was improved in later drawings from observation. It seems that not only can the perceptual memory be improved but that its improvement heightens actual observation as evident in drawings from direct observation.

The fact that, in this case, the activity was presented as a game obviously helped to introduce the children to the whole concept. The objects were received by chance, each child having a turn at a lucky dip. Later the finished drawings were matched to the objects also in a game situation. Such motivational tricks are not always necessary, but can be useful both in overcoming self-consciousness and in presenting as a metaphor an important experience which may lead to a realisation and understanding, as in this case, about visual memory. Memory is not purely visual. It too can take a form somewhere along the continuum of visual and haptic. The use of memory can be trained through the conscious teaching of its use applied to a number of situations.

Aesthetic perception may also be developed, not by the imposition of external aesthetic values of taste or fashion, but through drawing teaching methods which include the habit of appraisal or reappraisal of the drawn image as it emerges. The person who draws a line, rubs it out, draws another line and again rubs it out, demands fresh paper and then repeats the process is certainly in a crisis of confidence. The refusal to accept that line, then make another, to observe the relationship between the two and the picture space shows a chronic incapacity to perceive the aesthetic of these relationships. The ability to allow a dialogue to occur between the self and the drawing is important in creating an ability to take risks with the drawing.

I recently taught a group of 14- and 15-year-old girls for an afternoon. My group turned out to be the 'difficult lot'. Because this was to be a one off occasion I had chosen to ask the girls to participate in a project concerned with the illustration of Brecht poems, translated by a friend. The girls were in an agony of embarrassment. . . drawing and poetry! It was as if all the predictable responses had been rehearsed, 'Can't draw, Miss' 'What's it mean', 'Stupid!', etc, paper was grabbed, rubbers were in use within seconds. I asked them to forget the drawings and talk about the poem which I'd chosen, which was about the inappropriateness of schooling for some children when others were imprisoned by their longings for the most basic of needs, in this case a drink of water. To my surprise, once the girls had begun to grasp the meaning of the poem, their attention was captured and they discussed its implications with some insight. I asked them what kind of picture the poem conjured up in their minds. Everyone could see something and describe it. We talked about why the illustration had to be in black and white and about some of the practical printing problems and possibilities. A range of black and white illustrations to very different texts was shown to them and discussed in terms of qualities of line and style. I then invited them to choose from a good selection the type of drawing instrument they thought best for their idea. Everyone chose pencil. When I showed my disappointment they told me sensibly that this was in order to try out their ideas first and that when they had settled on a solution then they would chose another medium if need be, as eventually they all did. The work produced was in every case movingly sincere and in two cases showed a remarkable perceptive and personal response to the poem. Big difficulties had been encountered in representing the visualised ideas, but what I found so striking was that the girls had a very clear idea of where their skills were lacking. Because they felt that they had gained some new perceptions and knowledge they were able to accommodate to their lack of skill in other respects. Real aesthetic judgements were being made, about the relationship between the idea and image, between function and image, between the form and the content and the tools and the media used. Was this not evidence of aesthetic acumen developing?

Motivation

The development of perceptual, or any other, skill won't take place unless there is a conscious desire to learn. The creation of that desire is a major function of a teacher, and a major responsibility. For many adolescents, unless the teacher of drawing stimulates them to participate, drawing will cease to be an activity. This teaching role as facilitator is exercised from the initial impetus throughout the whole act. The provision of the appropriate stimuli may be the start, but motivation is needed to persist, to develop ideas, to refer to perceptual memories, to open oneself to new insights as the work progresses and to exercise and develop aesthetic sensibility. Teachers' success in this respect can be a reflection of their own enthusiasm for drawing which in itself acts as an inspiration.

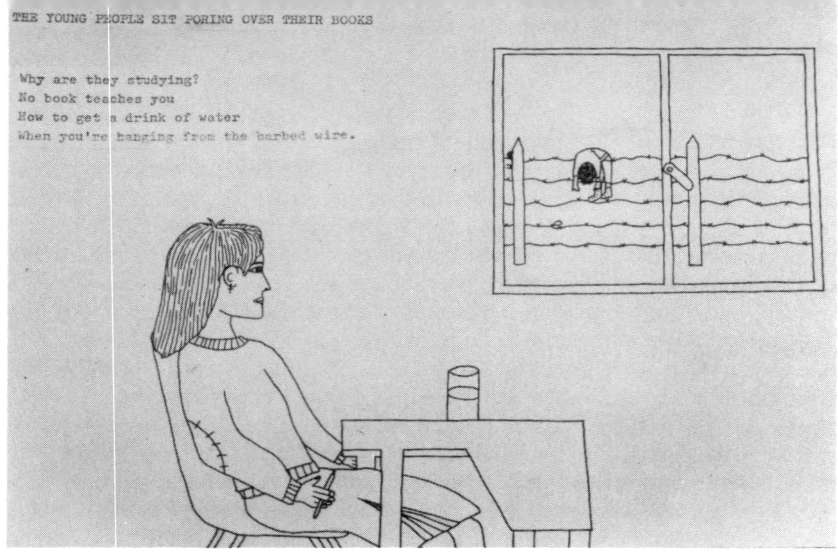

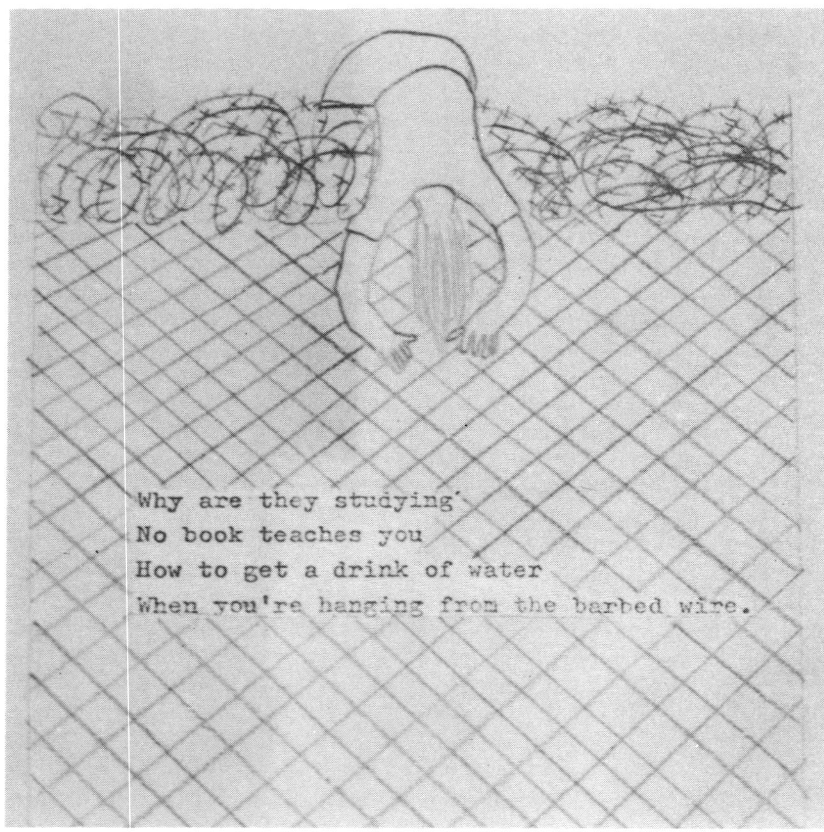

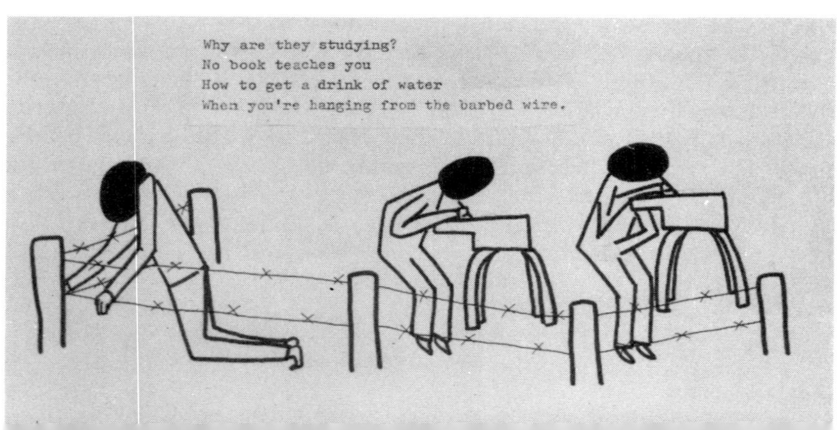

Three of the interpretations of the Brecht poem (14 years)

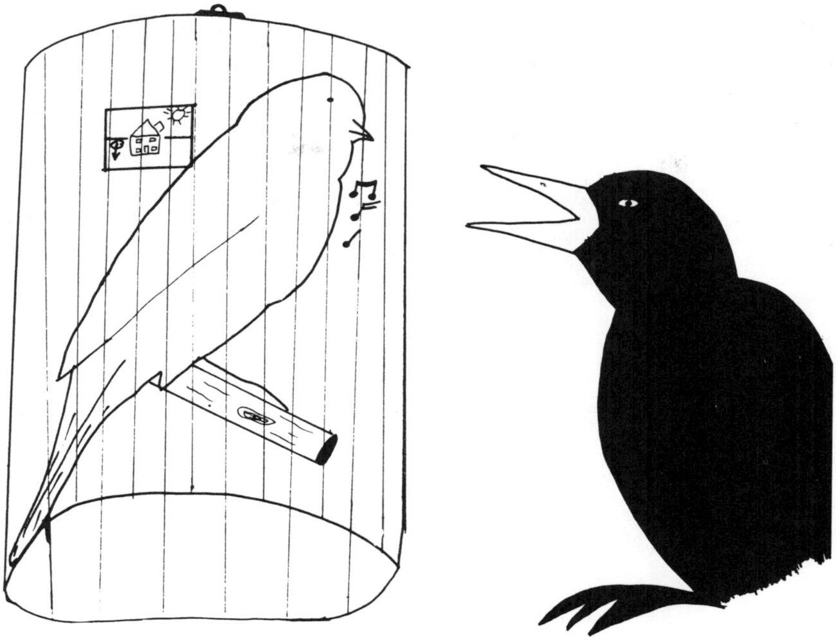

A 12-year-old's interpretation of

There once was a crow
Of crafty old age
Who heard a canary
Sing out from his cage:
Look here
You've got no idea
What art's about.
The crow snapped out:
If you couldn't sing
You'd be free like me
Bertholt Brecht

In the face of the limitations imposed by school structures, lack of facilities, large teaching groups, short lessons and so on, such enthusiasm is often difficult to sustain. Experienced teachers learn to know the kind of lesson which is likely to be successful. Sometimes there is a temptation to fall back on a previously successful formula. However, most thoughtful teachers learn to view with suspicion the repetition of successful lessons, for, when repeated, they may occur in a vacuum unconnected with any systematic build up of interest or expertise.

The enthusiasm of the teacher is a factor then in sustaining a stimulating climate for drawing. To keep that enthusiasm alive the teacher needs to be interested in the content of the work, and doing a drawing oneself can be a way to do that. Maintaining the interest of students is also a factor in keeping the teacher's own enthusiasm going. That being so it is necessary to ensure that there is awareness of the developmental range of the group to be taught, and that there is encouragement to respond to the task and to produce work that can be either visual or haptic. An opportunity to include a subjective response to the task even when its main function is analytical or objective needs to be present. The pupils' past experience should be considered, for the logic of the way the work is sequenced both short and long term is important. Above all the activity should be evidently worthwhile to teacher and taught.

Craft skills in drawing

The first section of this book 'Setting the scene' was concerned with the physical arrangements of the studios where drawing takes place. I have never seen a drawing studio as such in a school, though there may be a room called the Painting and Drawing Studio which often implies the place where a fine art approach is to be expected. This lack of special provision is understandable. Drawing permeates to so many art and design activities that to set

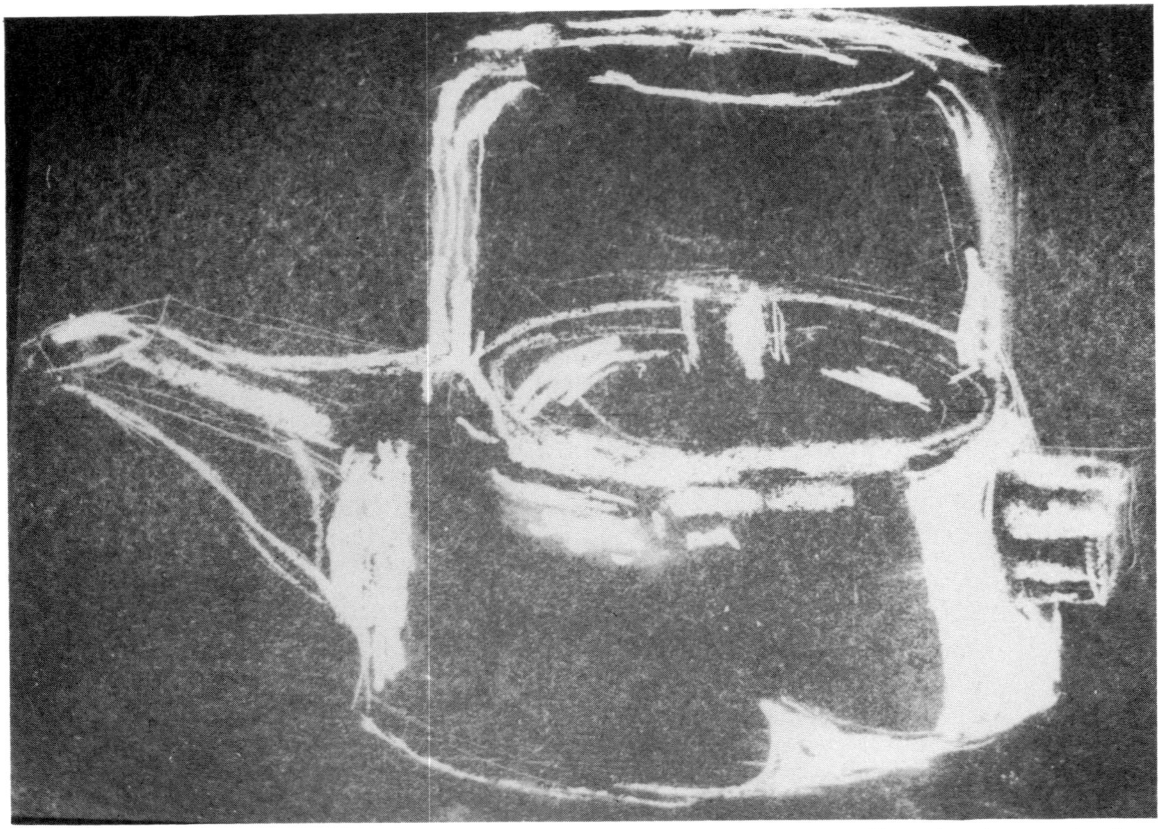

A study in tonality, soft media white conté on black paper

aside a special place for it may be seen as strange. Since drawing may be done without any special equipment or plant, no specialist area is thought to needed, unlike, say, sculpture.

But drawing has its own tools and procedures. There is a particular kind of learning pleasure, excitement and satisfaction in gaining control, be it motor or conceptual, of tools and processes. In the past much 'education' was focused on drilling skills into children and as a result the word, by association has got a bad name. The word, and the concept, has also become a dirty one in art and design circles. Another word which has become debased is 'craft' with its implications of deft manipulation of materials into objects, at best of traditional design but whose usage has often become debased into ornament, or of objects of poor or derivative design or of trivia. These words need to be cleansed of the residue of their recent usage, and reestablished as crucial aspects of art and design practice, and thus, by inference, of drawing. If we are to teach drawing in the belief that it is an essential form of the communication of thought and feeling then we would do well both to acknowledge that there are craft skills in drawing and to demonstrate how they relate to the other skill components of drawing.

To master a skill, its tools, materials and techniques need to be recognised and their various characteristics understood through practical experience. Language has a particular importance here. A grasp of the correct terminology can only be acquired by handling and using tools and materials. Acquiring the correct terminology can facilitate the act of drawing. For example, a person may have had a very good drawing experience with a charcoal pencil, a conté crayon, or a 6B pencil. There is a better chance that the skill or knowledge gained from that experience be retained and applied on other occasions, if the right language, ie 'conté crayon', 'charcoal pencil', have been learned as well. The naming of tools and materials correctly is an important habit and can be reinforced by careful labelling in storage areas and by the kind of display described earlier in 'Setting the scene'. The language of drawing of course goes beyond naming, but the more names are known, the more concepts about drawing can be formed. The greater the complexity of the concepts grasped about drawing, the more it is likely that such competence will increase.

The craft skills of drawing must always be acquired in context, that is in response to the idea to be expressed, otherwise there will be degeneration into the teaching of skills unrelated to function, idea or aesthetic considerations. There has sometimes been an attempt to introduce children to craft skills through work based on free experimentation with a medium or media. In my opinion such activities are for the majority of adolescents frustrating and counter productive. Gestural and media experimentation are sophisticated activities. Action painting, like improvised music, 'found' and concrete poetry are not the 'primal' and experiential stuff they're cracked up to be. Such experimentation requires enormous self confidence, and is usually most successfully done by artists whose craft skills are developed and publicly known. In fact that kind of experimentation can be counter productive in teaching, suggesting that craft skills don't count or are easily acquired. The essential relationship between image and craft skills is evident in all respects. For example, in the question of scale; a tiny drawing demands different tools from a very large one. Photo-realism is difficult to achieve with oil pastels, a range of tone from black to near white can only be achieved by softer media, drawing tools which produce colour differ in their colour quality according to their constituents. Content will determine form, and form may modify content. These are obvious statements, but only meaningful when based upon practical knowledge.

The teaching of craft skills can be approached from two main directions. The first would be one where the potential of one medium can be explored through a subject which lends itself to opportunities for that to occur. For example if the aim was to introduce the use of charoal it would be logical to align this to the exploration of tonality in describing volume of surface quality. The drawing of a portrait head under a strong spotlight may be an appropriate subject. The other direction is where a choice of media is made available for a given task, but that an important objective of the task is to carefully consider the choice of media used in terms of suitability, for example in the 'Sweets' project described later.

The physical manipulation of the tools and media of drawing have accrued some useful traditions based on trial and error. Why not teach these traditional tried and tested methods? I have observed so many young people abandon, even destroy an exciting piece of work over which many hours have been spent because of a mishap or a mistake. In almost every case this could have been avoided by tutoring in craft procedures, including work habits which minimise the likelihood of accident by showing ways of making simple repairs. Instruction is not necessarily an intrusion into the privacy of individual creation: it can be the very agent which facilitates it.

The formal skills of drawing

The most common tools and media of drawing are charcoal, conté, coloured and graphite pencils; oil, wax, pastel crayons; fountain, fibre, felt, stylo

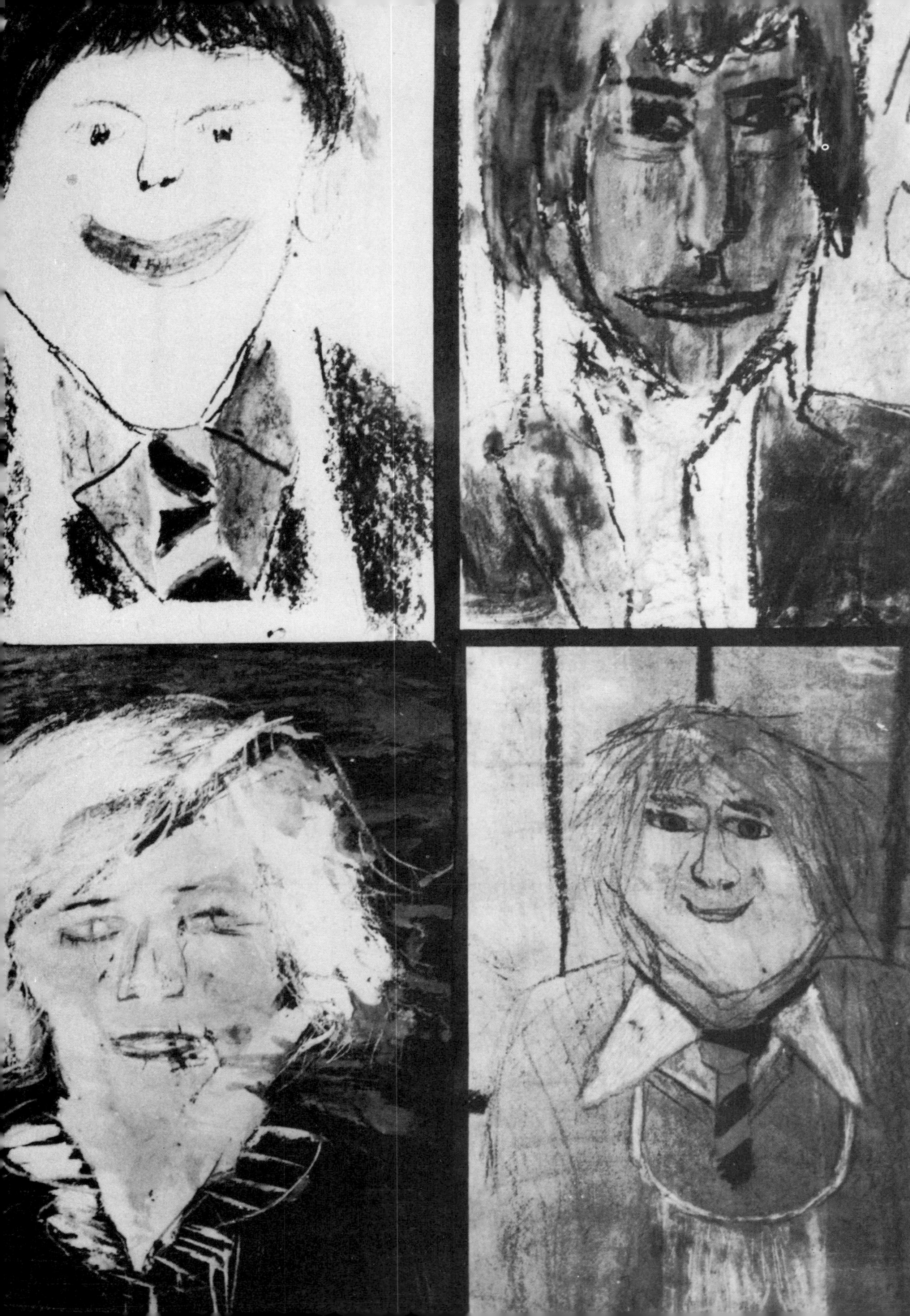

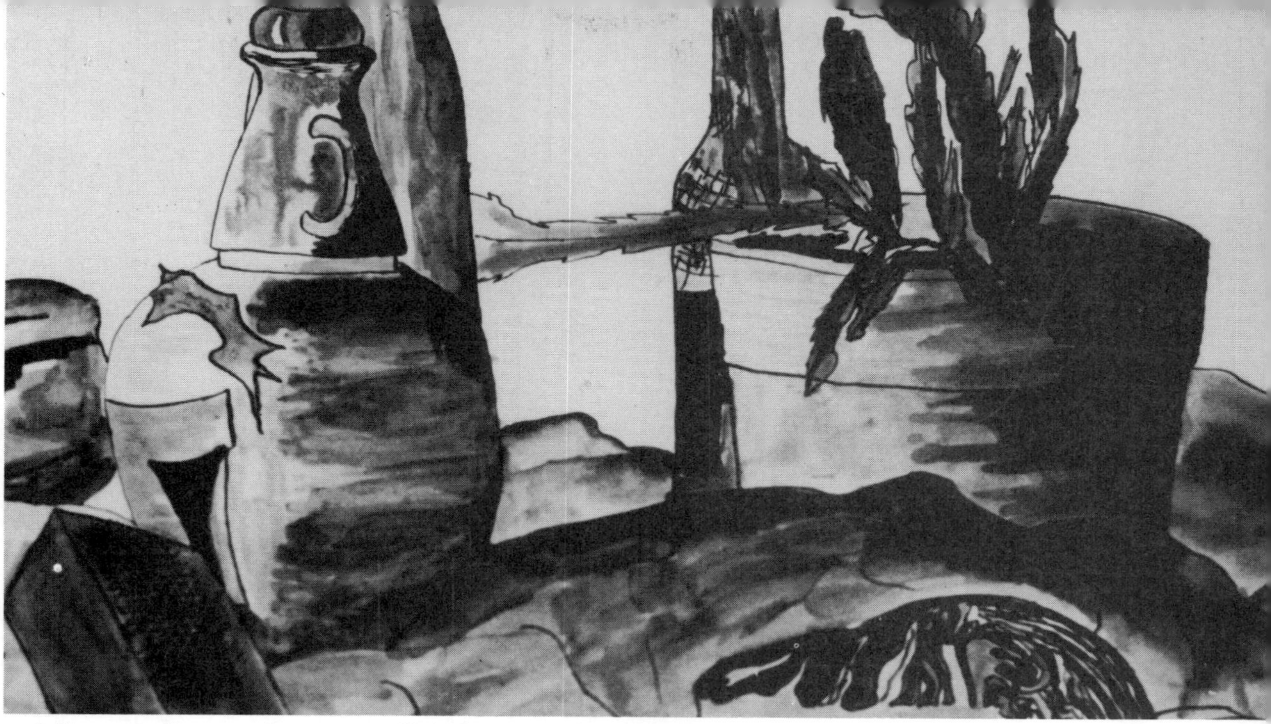

Detail of a pen and wash drawing – emphasis on tone

and dip pens; slip, mapping, crow quill, italic, script, five-line and copperplate nibs; fountain pen, stylo pen; coloured drawing, coloured film, Indian and drawing inks of many makes, and airbrushes. All produce lines, tones, and in some cases colour. Each one of them has a wide range of mark that can be explored and exploited. Used upon hot pressed, cold pressed, Ingres, Fabriano, Tumba, rough, heavy, medium, cartridge, Bond, Sugar, newsprint, wrapping paper the marks of each tool will vary. If any of these papers are dampened another kind of mark will appear. On some surfaces a widely differing quality of line may be explored, on another the surface or the tool will produce an unvarying line in tonal depth and weight. Some tools and surfaces don't marry well, the surface rejects the tool, or the tool scores into the surface and control is difficult, even impossible. The colour of the surface will affect the strength of the line made by the tools and, even more so, the tonal range. If the medium and the surface have colour there will be an even more critical effect on colour qualities and tonal range.

Some linear tools, such as a stylo pen, will produce a consistent *line* or a dot however they are held and no matter how weight is applied. Other tools such as a charcoal or graphite pencil are responsive to various ways of handling, producing from the fine to the thick line from the pale to the dark. Some media, such as hard pencils, cannot produce a truly black line, others, such as all soft pencils, can produce an opaque and intense black. Black conte or charcoal can produce the whole tonal range but even when carefully sharpened cannot produce a consistently fine, even line.

All these, and other, tools and media can be used to produce *tone.* The way in which they are employed to produce it will depend upon consistency and method of application. A fibre pen, a stylo or a dip pen, whatever the nib, cannot produce an area of consistent tone. An illusion of consistent tone can be produced through dotting or the use of lines placed closely together. The more lines to the square centimetre, the darker the tone. This technique is called hatching. The colloquial use of the term shading is really incorrect as shading can be produced by both hard and soft media. Hatching is a good word, almost onomatopoeic. It is a fascinating and enjoyable skill, especially

Opposite Portraits, 12-year-olds' bold and courageous use of various media

Soft media, charcoal conté chalk used for tonal study of various drapes (14 years)

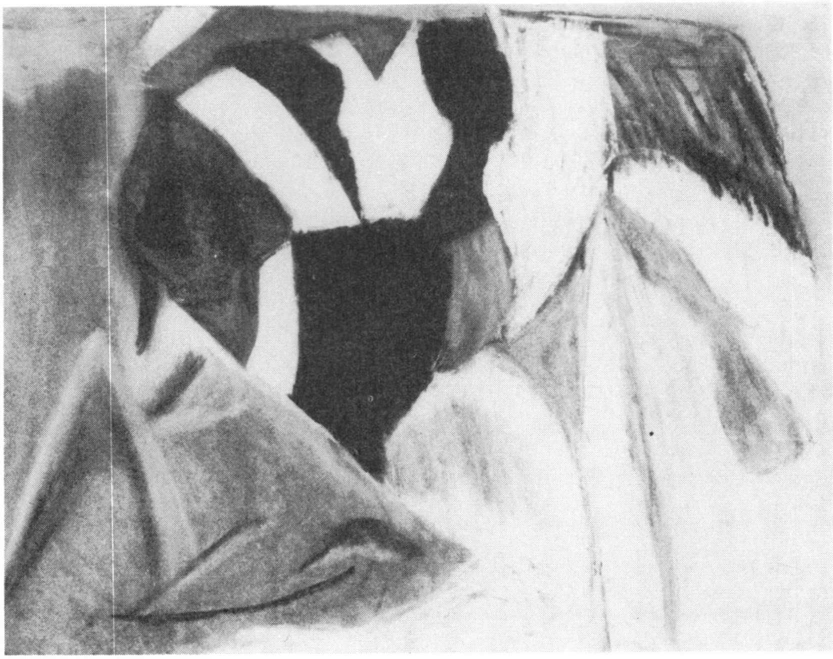

Unconventional treatment of a very traditional stll life devised to teach tonality and its use to describe form and space

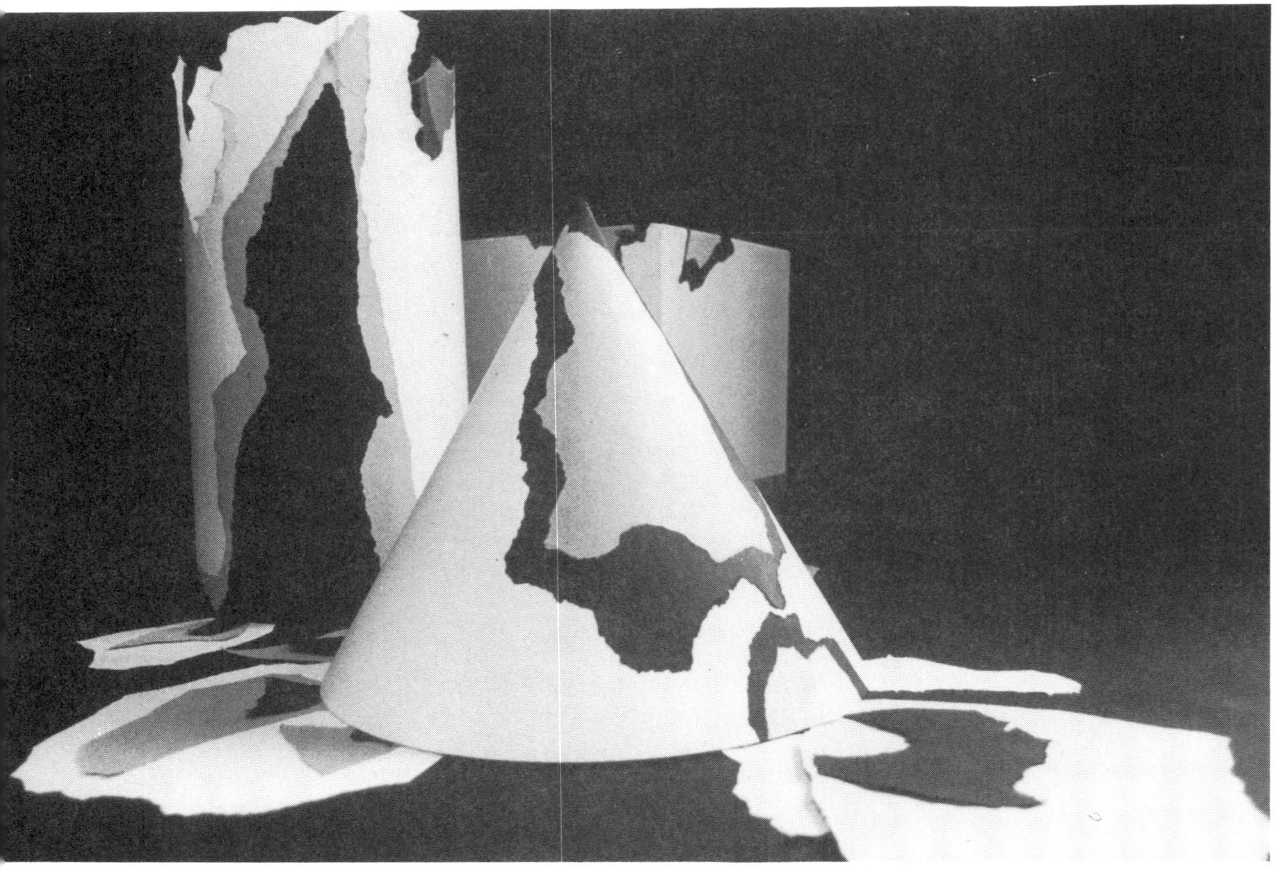

for the obsessive and meticulous. Hatching is most suitable for work on a relatively small scale, demanding as it does a gesture from the wrist rather than the elbow.

Tonality from softer media is usually produced by a rubbing technique. A soft medium such as charcoal, which when rubbed becomes powdery, can be made to produce quite large areas of either consistent tone or of tonal variations, both through the angle at which it is used or by rubbing with the finger, or a piece of cloth or sponge. Conté, because it contains clay and paste, wax crayons and oil crayons cannot be rubbed and spread by the finger, etc, though chalk and pastels can. Tone depends both on the amount of medium used and on the colour or tone of the medium. The amount of light allowed to sparkle through the tone will affect its quality. The roughness and surface quality of the paper will have some bearing on the opportunity to exploit this possibility. Sometimes applied pigment can be pulled away to lighten the tone, by a sharp tool, by a rubber, a piece of cloth or in the case of charcoal by pieces of bread. The angle at which chalk, conte, oil pastels and ordinary pastels are applied affects the quality of line and the tonal range possible. If the pigment is in the form of sticks, the side of the crayon can be used, if it is enclosed in a wooden pencil a more painstaking fine action is needed. Again the side of the colour is used, but, as very little of the side is exposed, the process will take longer, and aspects of the scale of the drawing will be affected. As ever, decisions about techniques should be normally based on suitability to the idea and function of the drawing. Such decisions must be based on knowledge of the flexibility and potential of the medium. Such knowledge, which may seem to be common sense, has to be learned as an integral part of learning to draw.

The way in which line and tone are produced in a drawing will vary according to the content of the drawing and the linear and tonal qualities most suited to that content, but they will also vary according to the scale of the drawing. Few miniatures are drawn with charcoal sticks, few murals with a mapping pen.

When drawing media have the added quality of *colour* another dimension is obviously added. Quality of both line and tone are affected by the colour in which they are drawn. This increases the complexity of the problems present in mastering these formal qualities, but there are bonuses too. Most of us enjoy the sensuous and descriptive quality of colour. It is curious that many people assume that drawing is devoid of it and should be confined purely to black and white. Drawing with dry colour is not only enjoyable but an excellent way to increase one's understanding of colour and its relationship to tonality. The range of colour quality to be found in dry colour is exceptionally wide, from the soft transparency of hard colour pencils, to the jolly and strong colour of good felt tips, to the sensuous, malleability of oil pastels when applied with weight and confidence.

The use of colour in drawing and the mastery of perceptual skills related to colour have obvious teaching potential. The distillation of our colourful world into black and white is an interesting exercise, but a curious one. The restriction to black and white obviously helps the perceptions to focus upon linearity and tonality in drawing. There is, however, no morality in restricting drawing to black, white and grey. Colour brings after all a new set of problems to be solved. Perhaps the convention, if it is one, derives from the cheapness and availability of black and white pigment for drawing. Certainly I feel that drawing with colour can be an excellent preparation for painting. It can open the perceptions, as already stated, to the different qualities of colour and, in the use of some media, to colour mixing and colour relation-

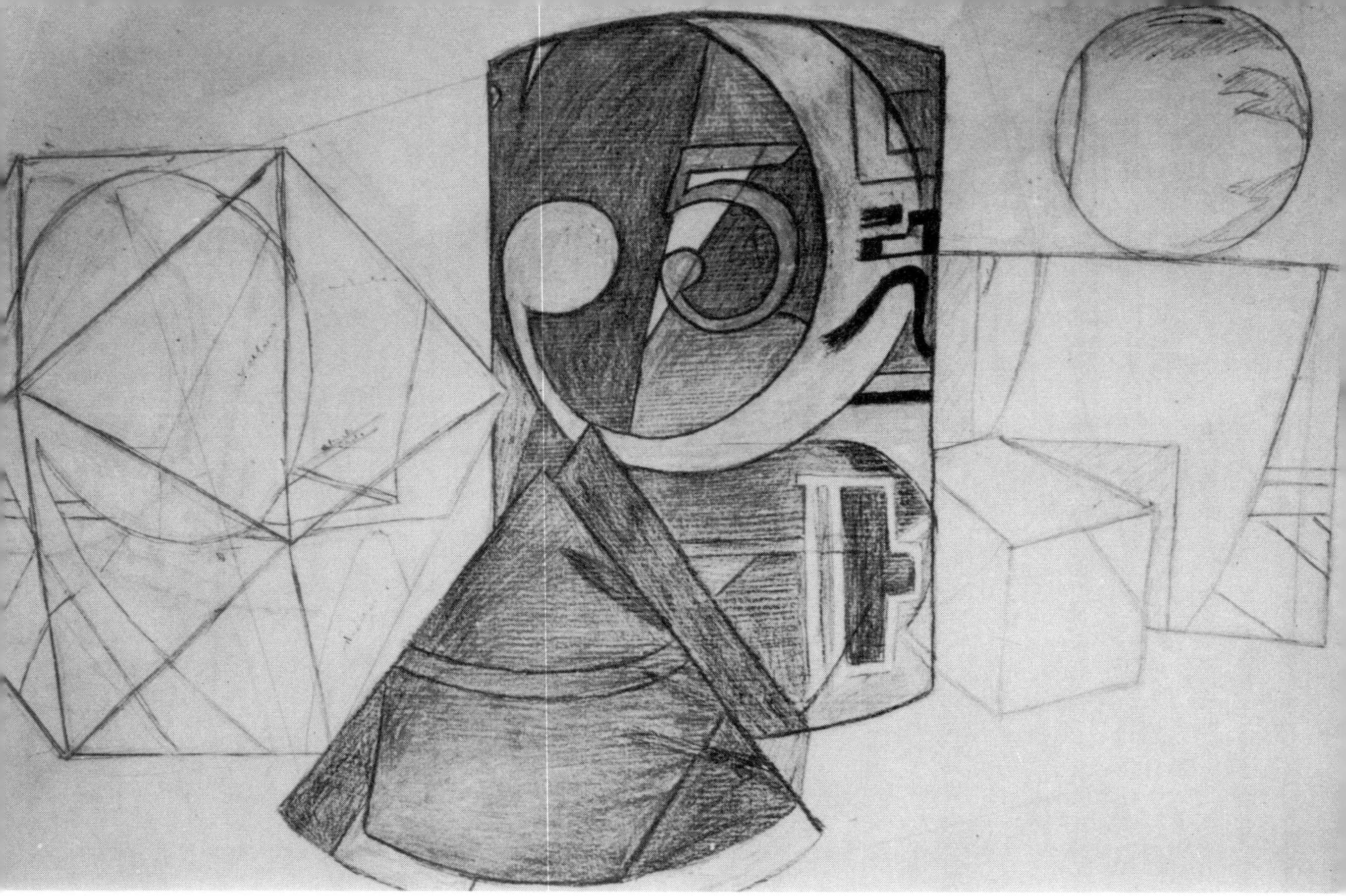

Another attempt to offer basic geometric forms for drawing, embellished in this instance by graphic patterning. These drawings were made in colour

ships. Perhaps most importantly since drawing tends to be more immediate, more direct, than painting, its use in drawing may allow for greater ease, for most people, in allowing a direct transference of perceptual sense experience to the making of images.

The coding skills of drawing

Deep satisfaction with a single line, a tone, a colour in isolation can be achieved through contemplation. Some artists have worked bravely to sensitise our perceptions to these formal basic elements of art. An essential impulse of drawing is to use these elements to describe and communicate.

The physical world of objects is made up of these elements, which are the particular province of the drawer, for it is this world which has provided the most powerful metaphors and symbols for ideas, for speculation and for communication in drawing. The ability to depict this physical world of objects in ways which are recognisable to others is an essential skill of drawing. Line, tone, sometimes colour are used to create two dimensional illusions of a three dimensional world. This transformation from one reality to another is curious and complex, but a teachable skill.

The physical world is brought to us through our senses which recognise and experience shape and volume, space and distance, time and movement and so on. Drawing also depicts these characteristics by creating illusions of them. The ability to create these illusions of space, volume and movement from line, tone and colour I have called the *coding skill* of drawing.

Objective or observational drawing is thought to be a way of teaching

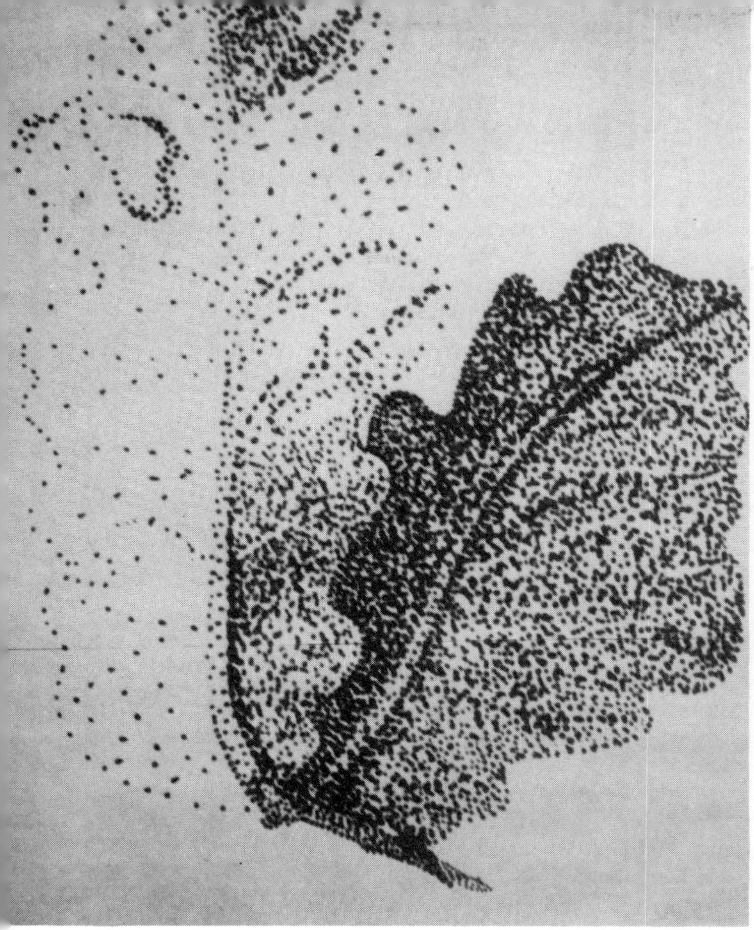

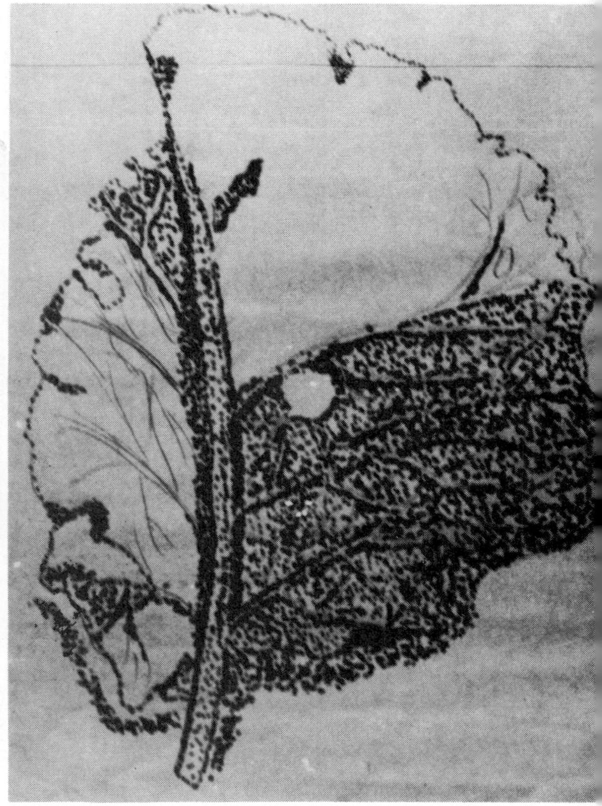

Left and above Dotting to create tone

this skill, as is also the Basic Design approach. While both have had a great deal of success, basic design can be too theoretical for many adolescents. The dynamics of visual form can be taught, understood and practised but as a basic 'syntax' of drawing it is not automatically transferred to a variety of drawing situations. The use of observation to understand volume, space and movement is logical and has the virtue of being pragmatic, but the observed reality is not the same as drawn reality, and any amount of observation doesn't teach how to learn the code which transforms one into the other.

Any methodology of teaching drawing may be successful if taught from rigorously worked out beliefs, from enthusiasm and imparted with conviction and care for the students. But an essential basis for teaching and learning drawing is that both parties, teachers and learners, understand the underlying principles about drawing from which content and method arise. Thus an approach to the teaching of drawing which is in anyway skill based, should by its practice and by the value systems, language employed, and references used, clarify the component skills, their relationship to each other and to the various functions of drawing. For many reasons drawing has been underrated compared to reading, writing and mathematics, the other symbolic systems of communication. Common too is a mystification of drawing as a particular form an expression available only to the gifted few.

While many people have expended a great deal of energy arguing that drawing is not merely representational and topographical, it can hardly be denied that the capacity to draw in a realistic and representational way is a skill which gives confidence. It also appears to be a base line from which abstract, diagrammatic and experimental drawing emerge. Does this mean that only those 'gifted' enough to draw representationally can eventually use drawing with great flexibility as a way of thinking, expressing and communicating, or, that if it is possible to teach young people ways in which representational drawing of the objective world may be acquired (as a way of making statements, descriptions of objects and even scenarios of objects) then more people would eventually be able to use drawing for a whole variety of purposes, thus enhancing the quality of their lives by their increased range of contact with ideas, feelings and people?

One common assumption is that one can learn to draw people, houses, trees, plants, cars, boats, etc, each as a separate practical skill. This probably arises from habits formed in the schematic stage where drawing is used, in part, to categorise and differentiate the physical world. The coding skill of drawing is applicable whatever the 'subject' of the drawing or the 'objects' which realise that subject. There is an important link between coding and the perceptual skill of drawing. Without the ability to observe and perceive the essence of objects, (their shape, relative size to other objects, the way in which they occupy space, their qualities of movement and weight, static and heavy, light and volatile, their proportions, their surface qualities) our ability to code these characteristics will be hampered.

The drawing skills related to *perception, craft* and *forms* are universal whatever the culture, although tonality is seldom or minimally used in some. Of course language related to the drawing skills must be culturally based also, for space, volume and movement are handled differently in places other than the West. The North American Indian, the Australian Aborigine, the Bengali, the Arab and the Yoruba handle these concepts differently from each other and from Western post–Renaissance artists. If then the concept of drawing codes is understood by pupils, then the codes or conventions used in other traditions should become more sgnificant to them. Indeed these other codes can be adopted and used by pupils according to the function of the drawing. Some young people may find that non-European codes are more natural to them, and they should be reassured that this is perfectly understandable and acceptable. On the other hand it would be grossly patronising to assume that children from families whose forbears are from other ethnic origins than Western Europe would naturally adopt drawing codes which may mirror the conventions of the art of their forbears. I know of no evidence to suggest that the use of a particular drawing code is innate. Such codes are obviously learned. While European art has changed and adapted its codes over the centuries two things do seem certain. The first is that the drawing code which derived from the Renaissance has persisted and the second that the majority of adolescents in our schools, whatever their social or ethnic origins, are fascinated by these codes and long for the skill to emulate them.

The codes here described are most commonly ascribed to representational drawing, but they are also applicable to drawing which describes space, movement or form in abstract, symbolic ways. Whichever way the codes are used it is unlikely that they can be adapted from one drawing to another unless the correct terminology and the related concepts have been both taught and learned. The concepts involved in the skill cannot be understood without the language, and the ideas behind the language cannot be divorced from the practical experience the language describes.

Surface or texture has been omitted from the list of space, volume and movement. It is not a logical category. Surface qualities, whether they be marking or texture, are evidence of structure, (eg wood grain), they can be evidence of weight, by association (eg shiny, like metal or glass). Surface can suggest space or distance (eg the stubble on a harvested field). It can suggest movement (eg ripples on water, clouds, wind through leaves). For these reasons it can fall into all of the three categories.

Once the various skills of drawing are recognised and their relationship to each other and to the whole image understood, the act of drawing would surely be demystified. Perhaps, too, young people would be more open to drawing activities if they knew that one of the objectives of the lesson or project was to give understanding or mastery of a particular drawing skill. If those objectives are mutually understood by the teacher and the learners then criteria may be established against which an individual can judge the level of success. He must understand that volume, space and movement are the codes used to build up a meaningful image, that line, tone and colour together in any combination, or alone, can create a two dimensional illusion of these, that a variety of tools and techniques exhibit varing degrees of efficiency in depicting line, tone and colour. The learner must also know that each tool and medium has its own interesting characteristics, and understand that certain behavioural states such as patience, persistence, the ability to use the senses fully in a disciplined fashion are needed. Then not only are the skills of drawing understood and seen as possible to master but also the process of drawing.

Once many media have been experienced, choice of what is most enjoyed by the individual or most suitable for the drawing of the individual's style is possible. If linearity, tonality and colour have been understood and practised then choice as to the formal emphasis in a drawing is possible. If confidence to show mastery of space, volume and movement is present then the ideational range of an individual's drawing is likely to be wider, more fluent, more flexible and more adaptable. If the pupil masters just one of the skills of drawing, confidence that another may be mastered is likely to follow. If the relationship between the skills is understood and demonstrated through the teaching, it can be realised that, in focusing upon one skill another may also be understood and possibly acquired. If there is a promise of time to be spent later focusing upon another of the drawing skills, disappointment about some aspect of the work will seem less threatening and defeating; if care has been taken to maximise the motivation of the students by allowing for identification with the drawing task through some aspect of interest such as subjectivity in response, then a total drawing experience is possible.

A skill-based approach to the teaching of drawing is often heavily criticised as being formulaic, at its worst offering a series of drawing tricks which 'close off' the pupil, making for less risk taking, less openness to perceptual experiences. Another criticism is that a skill approach turns drawing into a mechanical procedural activity which destroys the very nature of art which should be personal, creative and spontaneous. Another argument against it is the developmental one.

It is said that any teaching relating to space, or volume, for example, is likely to be pitched at the 'wrong' developmental stage for most of the individuals in the group. The teacher of drawing is likely to teach from a standpoint of sophisticated full linear perspective, the child still at a stage of 'primitive' perspective will be confused and made to feel inadequate. This sort of situation certainly happens and is a reason why many teachers feel unhappy about tackling objective and observational drawing.

All of these criticisms should be taken very seriously, for if the teaching of the skills of drawing is done without real understanding, or taught in a way which is divorced from the other aspects of drawing, then it can fall into these traps and be dangerous.

One answer to the formulaic criticism is this: there is a great difference between the child fixing on and repeating a few drawing tricks which have at some point been admired, but which have degenerated into a conforming formula, and the offering to a pupil of a strategy for suggesting, for example, how to show distance through overlapping, which hadn't been realised before. There is the likelihood that overlapping will appear with some regularity in the child's work for some time as a way of showing distance. With careful teaching a situation will arise where either the child becomes dissatisfied with this strategy and asks for an elaboration of it, or will find one autonomously. Alternatively the teacher can elaborate overlapping through a further project where space and distance are central to the idea. Any process or concept we teach can degenerate into a trick if it's taught out of context or without understanding. Nor must we be too hasty in labelling an aid given as a trick. We are all users of such tricks. For example children who are experiencing difficulty with problems of drawing the figure may be taught how to do proportional measuring. They may previously have been told that the vertical length of the head fits five or six times into the body. That rather crude piece of information may have helped them to see why their previous standing figures were grossly 'out of proportion'. Now they are discovering that when they wish to draw the body seated foreshortened or twisted this previous formula doesn't work. At this point proportional measuring might help – it can be a way to check an observational drawing. It is certainly not a water tight formula for figure drawing, or even for getting the proportions right, but can be a useful perceptual device at the right time and in the right sequence.

The teaching of the skills of drawing demands an active teaching role. A teacher said recently 'School art is school art and we shouldn't fool ourselves it's anything else'. What she meant was that in school there are demarkations of time and space. Drawing is taught to groups of people of a given number, the demands of the school value system and the public examination system are ever present. Such factors will affect the way we teach and the emphasis in the teaching. Many teachers feel that these conditions mitigate against their sincerely held beliefs about the personal and individual nature of art activity. These teachers may also fear that any emphasis on the skills of drawing can interfere with the very essentials of art.

These teachers would largely subscribe to the belief that skills should be introduced when a felt need arises on the part of the pupil. The teacher I quoted was pointing out that such an approach is hardly possible given the institutional structure of the school.

The other approach, which perhaps may be better accommodated within the administative constraints of the school, tends toward a belief that without the confidence that the mastery of a range of drawing skills engenders, ideas can be stultified and their expression frustrated. This second approach suggests a drawing curriculum structured on a conscious build-up of drawing skills. This would be a response to the critics of a skills approach who fear the mechanisation of drawing so taught.

The developmental argument against a skill based approach to the teaching of drawing relates to the last objection as well. While younger children do seem motivated to use drawing freely as a means of personal expression, very few adolescents do. We have discussed the likely reasons for this earlier and the consequent need to present drawing as having other important additional functions. Lack of confidence, self criticism, fear of the criticism of others makes the free and public use of drawing as a vehicle of self expression and communication very unlikely for most young people except in the context of very careful and protective teaching.

As far as the danger of making a mismatch of the skills offered to the conceptual stage of pupils is concerned, this would be a danger whatever the approach. This is not to say that skill based teaching does not have particular dangers. It would be a grossly insensitive teacher who imposed a package of 'right' and 'wrong' methods of drawing. In an informed skill based curriculum there would be an understanding of the developmental range to be found in any teaching group. As a result the teaching methods employed would take care to avoid presenting any child with a situation where there is conceptual inability to meet the task.

Teaching can play a part in facilitating the move from one conceptual stage to the next. It very often does, but those children who can't assimilate the new concepts at the time have good mechanisms for dealing with them, and, in any case, new concepts can be understood on a variety of levels. For example many teachers have found that the rules of linear perspective can be relatively easily taught to children with a variety of levels in art skills. These rules are after all logical and clear. Such lessons are usually compellingly fascinating, drawings are made which follow the rules and a good time is had by all. Very few children however can subsequently apply these rules in other drawings. Most will abandon it, some will continue to struggle with it, trying to apply it and losing heart because it doesn't meet the spatial needs of current drawings. A few will be able to understand and assimilate the rules, apply them and elaborate them for themselves. Like other aids toward the skill of depicting space in drawing, linear perspective has very limited value, certainly for younger adolescents it can do more harm than good since it can lead to more frustration, not less.

The reason for categorising these skills is not to enable them to be taught in unrelated isolation but to give us and our students a conceptual framework against which to see the components of the act of drawing and to demonstrate that these separate skills or components are not mysterious talents but skills that can be learned. The methodology of how they are to be taught and learned is the creative act of every teacher, for the other factors to be considered are not only the practical ones of time and numbers but also the identity of that group, the needs of the individuals within it, their past experience of drawing and the personality and interests of the teacher.

4 Some skill-based projects

It may be helpful to describe some practical projects where there was an emphasis on drawing skills in the terms described in the last section. This may demonstrate how, even when the project is designed to draw attention to one of the skills of drawing and to give the opportunity to master some aspect of that skill, all the other skills of drawing are exercised and in some cases equally developed. The common consideration in setting up these projects was to try to create as high a level of interest in the work as possible. Any teaching would aim to do that. The way in which people develop an interest when entering into an activity obviously depends on factors to do with creating interest and attention. It also depends on the people to be motivated and what the teacher knows of them.

The sweets project

The first project was done with a group of 13- and 14-year-olds. The children were visiting a college to participate in a drawing project and this was their first visit. It was felt important to create a welcoming intriguing and unthreatening atmosphere but one where there was the expectation of serious work seriously taken. There was to be an emphasis on two of the skills of drawing, the *craft* skills and the *coding* skills. The craft emphasis was to be concerned with the choice and use of tools and techniques according to the scale of the drawing. The coding skill was to be concerned with the depiction of aspects of movement.

Sweets was chosen as the subject of the drawings and to this end a variety of sweets of many kinds were collected together. Each child was asked to make at least one small drawing of a sweet and at least one large drawing of a sweet. The scale was controlled up to a point by the provision of paper cut to appropriate scale.

The first part of the lesson was concentrated on the craft skill of choosing appropriate media and tools for the scale of drawing, but as sweets were available they were handled and observed, in some cases eaten! The perceptual skills were being exercised.

Once the drawings were made and there was a collection of both small and large drawings, they were cut out. A huge paper background had already been stuck together and on this the neck of a sweet jar was drawn. The large drawings were to be arranged as though falling out of the jar onto a surface. The small drawings were to be arranged as though crammed into a cellophane bag. A 'cellophane bag' made from perspex had been cut out previously. The group discussed in some detail the two tasks. They observed the actual sweets falling from a jar. They experimented with the possible compositions and came to a collective decision about the two solutions. The contrast between the two types of movement was discussed and some relevant terminology intoduced, such as 'static' and 'dynamic'. Care was taken to use differentiated names for the media, oil pastels, chalk pastels, fibre tip, stylo, colour pencils, cartridge paper and so on.

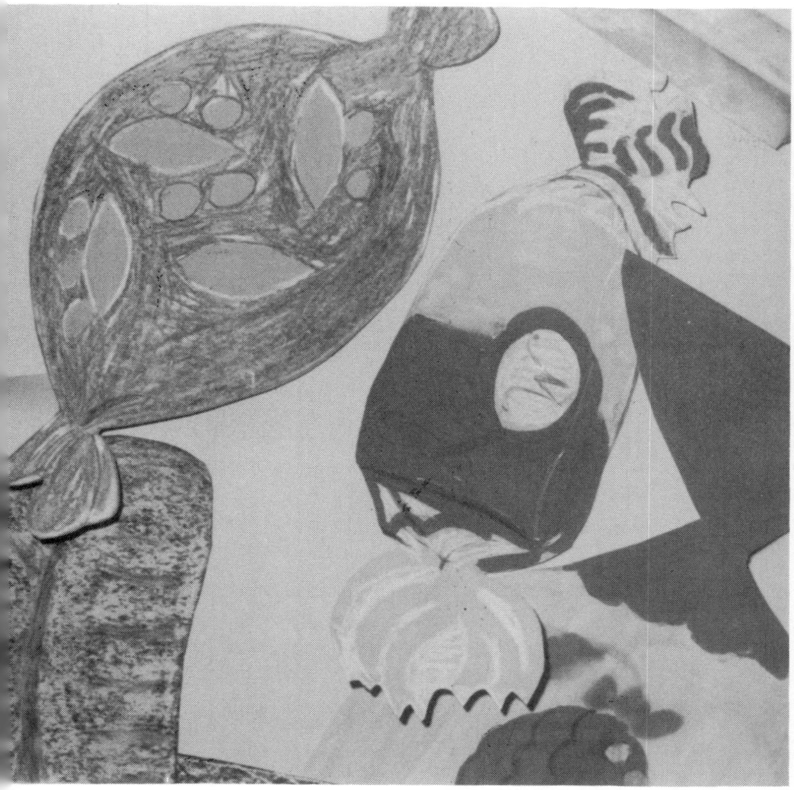

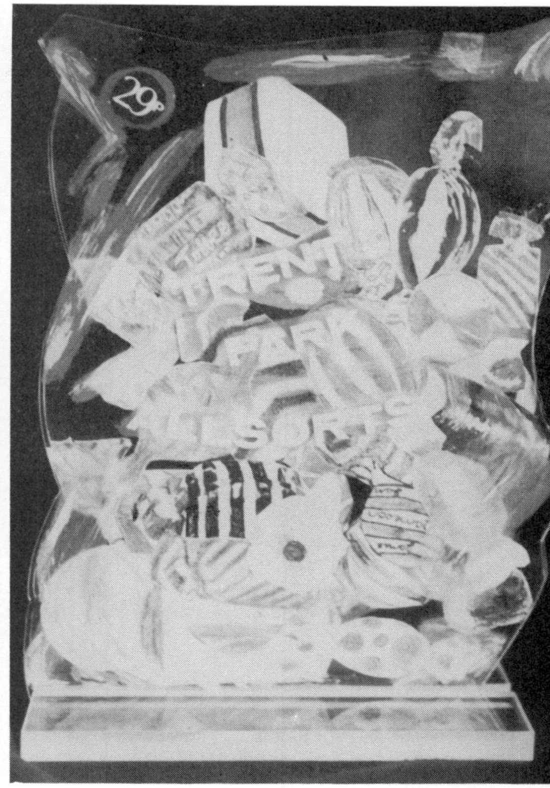

Left Part of the large sweets drawing

The finished arrangement of the tiny sweets drawing

The illusion of movement was created through trial and error but the children had discovered that grouping, overlapping and the use of diagonally placed objects gave the image more dynamism. As they described it, it looked 'more real'. This discriminatory activity was partially a coding operation, partly a perceptual one, where aesthetic decisions were made.

The space project

This project was done with the same group of children on the second meeting. Here the skills to be developed were the *formal* skills and the *coding* skills. The particular coding skill was the creation of the illusion of volume, ie three dimensional shape in a drawing. The formal skill used to achieve this was to be through tone in particular.

As this was only the second visit there was still the need to motivate the children by both reassuring them as well as by capturing their interest. 'Space' is commonly thought to intrigue young people, and *Star Wars* was the current film craze at the time. The subject also was thought to be suitable in that it gave the opportunity to use the basic shapes of the sphere, cone and cylinder rather than other more complex objects, but in an intriguing and 'imaginative' way. A spacescape was produced very simply from boxes and card, all was painted white, given a backcloth and spot lights were put into place.

It was hoped to demonstrate the difference between a linear drawing and a tonal drawing. The children were therefore asked to make a line drawing of the spacescape. This they then traced onto tracing paper and the tracings put to one side.

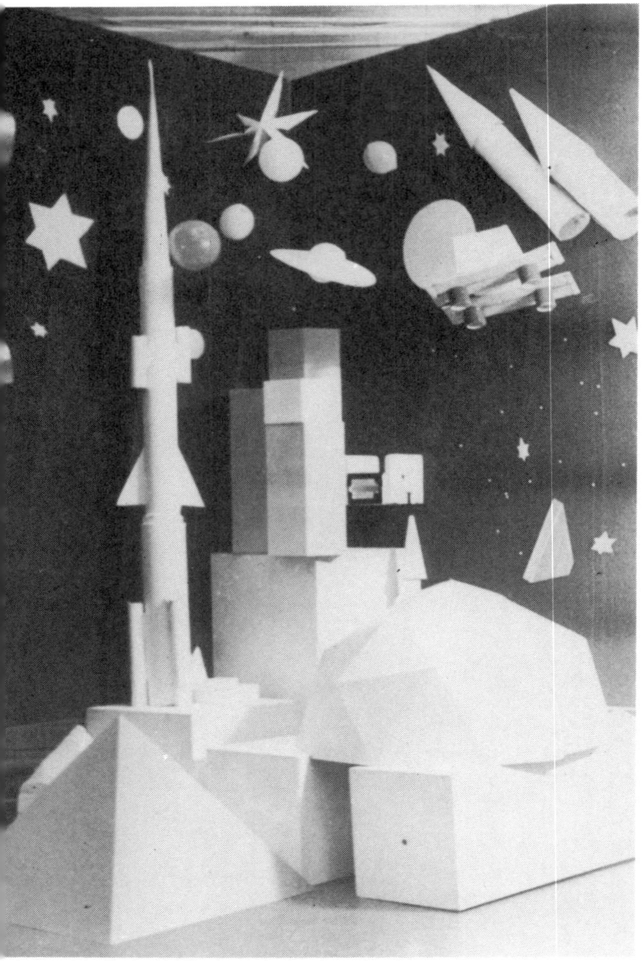

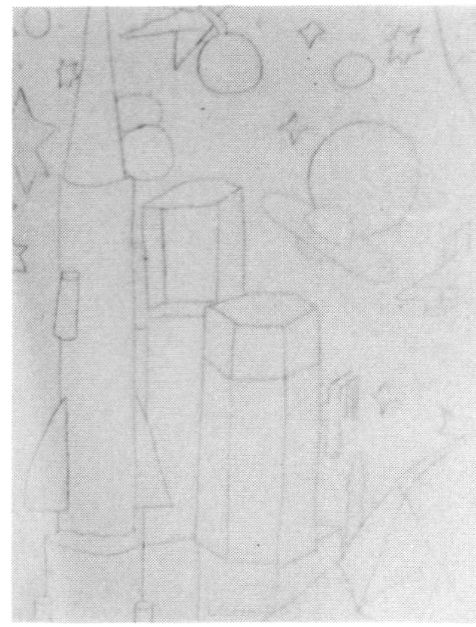

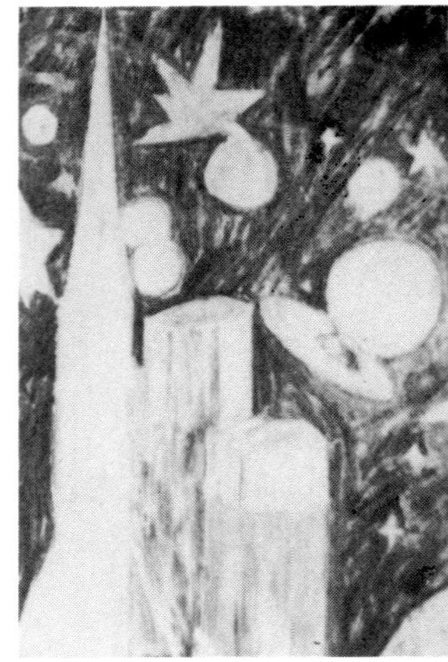

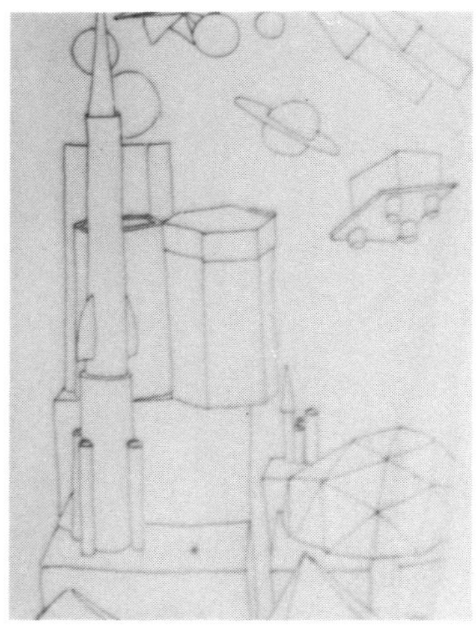

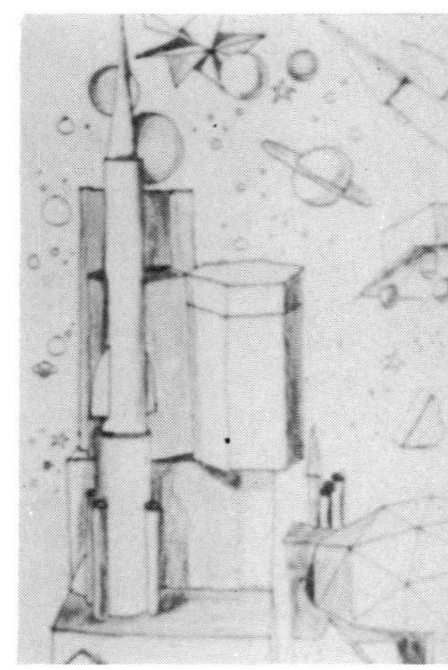

Above The space scape from which the drawings were made

Centre Two of the drawings showing the tracings of the linear treatment and *right* the final drawings using tone

Then the spot lights were turned on and the children asked to look carefully at how the shadows described the shapes of the objects in the space-scape. They continued their drawing by putting in the shadows and trying to see how the tone darkened as it moved away from the light. At the end of the lesson the finished 'tonal' drawing was compared to the linear tracing and they were asked to consider whether or not the addition of tone had helped to describe the shapes or volume of the objects more. Indeed the distinction between shape and volume was pointed out. All the skills were again being brought to bear in this exercise; perception and language, as well as the emphasised ones of form and code. The craft skills were included. The children considered a choice of most suitable linear tools for the first drawing, none smudging because of the tracing, then softer media for the second drawing to give more tonal variety.

The media available for this project had been limited thinking this would help the concentration on tone and volume, but, although the point had been made, certain problems were encountered. On the craft side it was found that the charcoal on offer to the children was a medium unknown to them, as a result they found using it difficult because they didn't understand how soft it is. Involuntary smudges are counter productive in a project where the careful use of controlled tone is important. Also the complexity of tonality had been underestimated. Although the spot lights helped by emphasising the shadows and by dramatising the situation, they also created cast shadows and reflections off the shiny card used to make the cylinders and cones. A careful diagnosis of the results of this lesson could have produced a useful series of follow-on projects using tonality or volume as a central teaching emphasis.

Many of the children felt that they had learned a great deal from this session however, and it's interesting to note that the group were very noticeably exhausted at the end of it, presumably because their level of concentration had been so great.

The circus project

This single session project aimed to concentrate on the coding skills relating to volume and movement. In particular it tried to help the children to understand the importance of proportion both within a shape, in this case human and animal shapes, and comparatively.

The depiction of different types of movement by people and animals alone and in space was the other consideration of the project.

Because the concepts involved were complicated it was decided to produce aids for this project. Lay figures of jointed animals and humans were prepared. Butterfly clips were used at the joints so that the maximum amount of articulation was possible. Figures were made in profile and frontally.

The subject of a circus was chosen as it gave the opportunity to use many different types of animals and also many human types, such as children, adults, tall muscular, short muscular, fat, thin, lithe, athletic and so on. Everyone in the group was to make a figure chosen from a category, such as clown, bareback rider, trapeze artist and so on. A lay figure was chosen whose physical type was best suited to their chosen category. This was the first stage of the activity, ie consideration of correct proportional type related to that choice.

Next came the opportunity to experiment with the lay figure. By taking it through a movement and drawing round the figure at each stage it was hoped to show how the alignment of the different parts of the body goes through a multitude of permutations to achieve one movement. The use of the short cut of using the lay figure as a template was to demonstrate this and also to

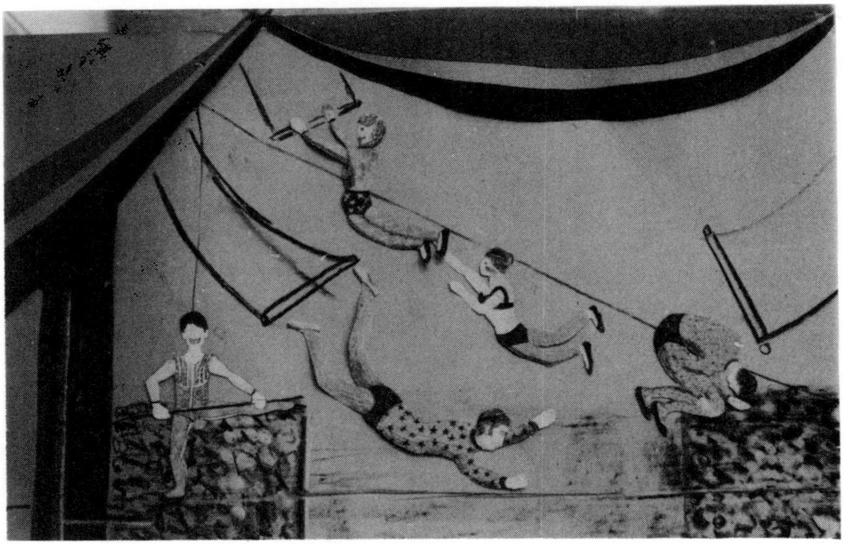

A section of the completed circus drawing

show how a drawing, which is static, initially, can create the illusion of movement.

After experimenting with the figure a movement was chosen which would be most characteristic of that figure performing in a circus. It was drawn with the help of the lay figure, cut out and placed on the circus backdrop already prepared. This placing was another stage in the activity for decisions had to be made about the composition of the total picture. The space of the circus tent was suggested partly by the placing of the characters according to their size and by drawing in highwires, trapezes, etc.

Different tools and media were used at different stages of this project. The choice of medium related to the stage of the drawing. The early experiments with the lay figure were done, by most of the children, with felt tips as they wanted to get a clean outline. When they came to draw the figure to cut out, they used pencil in order to avoid a strong outline. Details of clothing tended to be done with small but strongly coloured media; details of the circus tent were done boldly with coloured chalks or a large brush and ink. Thus decisions were made based on appropriateness of media to scale and to the idea of the drawing. Aesthetic considerations were made at every stage of the work. Formal skills were exercised – line was used in the first part, colour was seen to be important for a circus, then, as the work was assembled, it was realised that there are strong spotlights in the circus, and some children tried to suggest this by applying tone.

The little and big project

Another project was designed to introduce the importance of scale when describing space. In this project there was a very specific emphasis on a particular coding skill, ie the creation of space in a drawing. To make the point palatable it was presented in the form of a game.

The children were asked to make two lists. One was of the biggest plants, animals, insects, birds, they could think of, the second was of the smallest of these things. So, at this early point, they were already thinking in terms of scale.

They were then invited to choose one thing from the 'biggest' list, another from the 'smallest' list. These two creatures or plants were to form the two major characters in their drawing, but the smallest of the two was to be drawn in the foreground of the drawing, and the largest on an horizon line drawn across the paper somewhere above the centre. The visual joke would be that the drawing of, say an elephant on the horizon could be very much smaller than that of a fly in the foreground. Thus far the point had been made about relative scale and distance.

The next phase of the drawing was to complete the drawing of the space from the foreground to the animal or plant on the horizon line, and beyond if need be, keeping to relative scale and using the drawings done as reference points. We were surprised how well this was achieved. It seemed a difficult concept to explain, but the start of the drawing seemed to have made a strong enough conceptual impact to enable most of the children to apply it throughout the drawing. I suppose such a start quite dramatically places the drawer in direct spatial relationship to two points within the picture plane.

The perceptual skills were obviously at work here. As no direction about the use of tools or medium were given, but a range was made available, it was interesting to see how each person tended to choose media with which they felt confident. This seems to be a sensible craft decision since the drawing demanded concentration on the use of a new code.

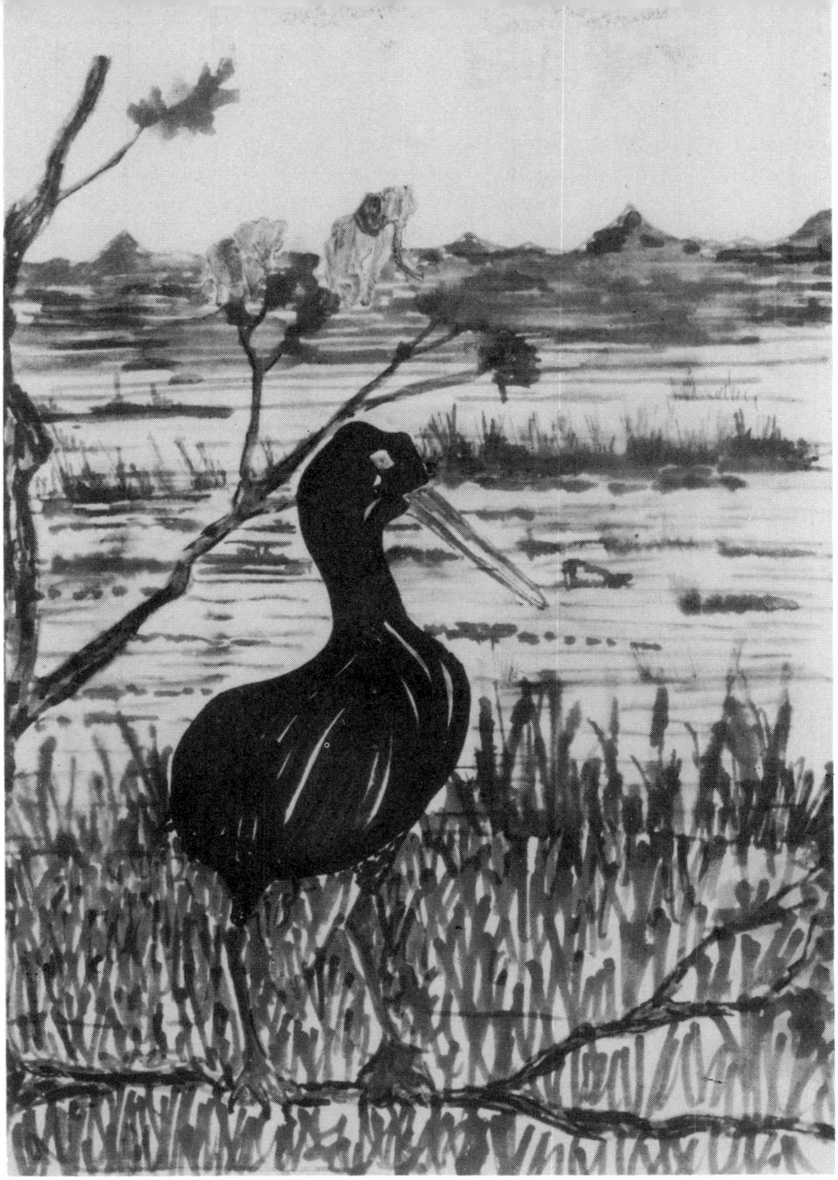

A little-and-big drawing

A colour project

This project was done with a small group of 12- to 13-year-old girls over five sessions, one week apart. The aim here was described as primarily 'enjoyment of colour'. What occurred was an emphasis on developing the *perceptual* skills in relation to the qualities of observed colour, and as a result craft, formal and coding skills were very tangibly developed.

By offering these girls a good choice of colour drawing media, oil and chalk pastels, coloured pencils, coloured fibre tips, wax crayons and laying them alongside the objects to be drawn, (in the first instance a luscious array of fruits) it was hoped that they would make a visual link between the colour qualities of the fruits and those of the media placed beside them. This happened up to a point, but on the first occasion, where there was some nervousness about performance, there was a greater tendency to choose the medium each individual found most tractable.

This first cornucopia of colour was too difficult for the girls to handle, in other words it was perceptually indigestible, so for the next two sessions there was an increasing paring away and focusing down upon the local colour of the fruit, first by each individual drawing a cross-section of one chosen fruit, then by each child drawing one section of an orange which segment was later joined with the drawings of others to form a whole orange. Each of these sessions lasted a little over an hour, and the concentration for the whole of that time was on feeling the colour drawn, both through the sensing of the fruit and the translation of the colour in the drawing through the media.

The fourth session moved away from fruit. A small colour relief was made from card and coloured paper, and this was to be the model from which the girls would draw. Their confidence with the media and techniques was now very assured. Almost without exception they all chose to use oil pastels which have the same glossy quality as the coloured paper used in the relief. Spontaneously, as the drawings were completed, they were cut up and joined together, prompted no doubt by the joining together of the segments of the orange the week before.

It was extraordinarily pleasurable to see this group of girls enjoying the colour they had created and to hear them discussing how the colours had spatial qualities, how given that yellow against that red, the red recedes, how even opaque media can have transparency in colour, how certain shapes in certain colour can turn at an angle away from the picture plane.

The final week of this short project was devoted to a still life drawing of a jug of flowers, but again concentrating on the colour. The attack was a great contrast to the tentative colour of the first session. Equally pleasing was the individuality of every person's drawing.

Perceptual projects

New perceptions very often create the motivation to draw. This belief was behind another five-session project with second-year girls and boys. It was felt that to give the children the opportunity to create an environment themselves, admittedly from given objects, in this case tailors dummies and dead trees with a few hats and scarves, they would be motivated to make drawings. The children did enjoy setting up the environment, but when it came to the drawing, they sat back from what they had arranged and each selected a tree from which to make a rather tentative drawing.

A new perceptual experience is not enough. It seems the skill to use this experience and transform it into an image through media, forms and codes has to be taught. As a result of the lesson learned, on the second session the same objects, ie the dead trees and the tailors dummies were used again, but this time red and green coloured spots were thrown on them to create cast shadow both on the back cloth and also across each other. Since colour was an important ingredient of this new perceptual experience, only fine coloured tools and media were made available. The children were asked to draw shadows as well as objects. While still tentative, these drawings began to show real observation and less worry about producing an 'acceptable' drawing. The third week again the trees and dummies were used but with striped clothes thrown across them to help describe the form. As it had been noticed that a common characteristic of the drawings of the previous week had been an inability to compose the drawing within the picture space, everyone was provided with a card 'viewfinder' of exactly the same dimensions as the paper. This produced two benefits, it helped the children to focus their perceptions on a manageable part of the total group, and it helped them to think in terms of composing their drawing.

Unusual lighting had been a perceptual aid in these two sessions, the spatial relationship between the group to be drawn and the group drawing it had also been considered. On the first session it had been hoped that the children would sit amongst the environment they had made. Their learned convention was that you sit back from the thing you draw. On the second and third sessions the furniture and materials had been arranged in such a way that the drawer was in close proximity to the things drawn. On the fourth and fifth session new perceptual stimuli were introduced in the form of music related to the new objects now offered as still life groups.

The work became freer and freer, the use of the picture space more confident, also the use of a range and mix of media common. Colour, line and tone were employed according to individual needs and the demands of the group of objects to be drawn. Movement was not overtly explored, but space and volume were.

The constant demand made by this teaching situation, which was always set up in the same room and same part of the room, was perceptual attention.

A great deal of ingenuity is demanded of the art teacher in training the perceptual skills. Adolescents are very distractable by nature and especially at 14, 15 and 16 years old. This is unfortunate when we realise how important the perceptual skills are in observational drawing and thus to success at 'O' level. It does seem an inescapable part of the job of teaching drawing to devise ways of drawing attention to the formal qualities of what we see: line, tone, colour, and to aspects of space, volume and movement.

One can experience some sympathy with the Victorian and Edwardian drawing instructional methods of presenting students with white cubes, spheres, cylinders and cones in order to demonstrate volume, even though we are horrified by the arid, academic, and boring prospect of spending hours upon the drawing of such unengaging objects. We long to give our pupils experiences which are enjoyable, believing that given a subjective identification with the object, lively and committed drawing will result.

If the skill components of drawing are understood by our pupils, however, and they are motivated anyway to acquire these skills, they are likely at mid-adolescence to accept drawing situations which demand a perceptual engagement which is analytical. Subjectivity can still be present in more ways than one. A personal desire to master a skill is subjective in one sense, and a very acceptable motivation.

Since an important aspect of teaching drawing to adolescents is concerned with developing the ability to draw accurately from observation, and since in any case such an ability benefits all other aspects of drawing it is worth making such drawing experiences as beneficial and enjoyable as possible.

Enjoyment of our perceptions suggests aesthetic pleasure. Such pleasure has little to do with ideas of beauty, taste or fashion. It is more concerned with the pleasurable shock or jolt of a new realisation and understanding and, in this context, confidence that what has been perceptually understood can be translated into the form of a drawing. If the child understands the means whereby this may be achieved (line, tone, colour), and the two dimensional illusions (volume, space, movement) which must be created through these means, then there is confidence that the perception can be utilised and transformed. This suggests first that the skills of drawing are truly interdependent for the mastery over a new perception depends on confidence that the other drawing skills may be deployed. It also illustrates how important it is that the pupil has a conscious understanding of the skill components of drawing.

My belief is that a truly skill-based approach to drawing is one where it is understood and accepted by everyone concerned that the function of the drawing project in hand is to concentrate on developing perception, craft,

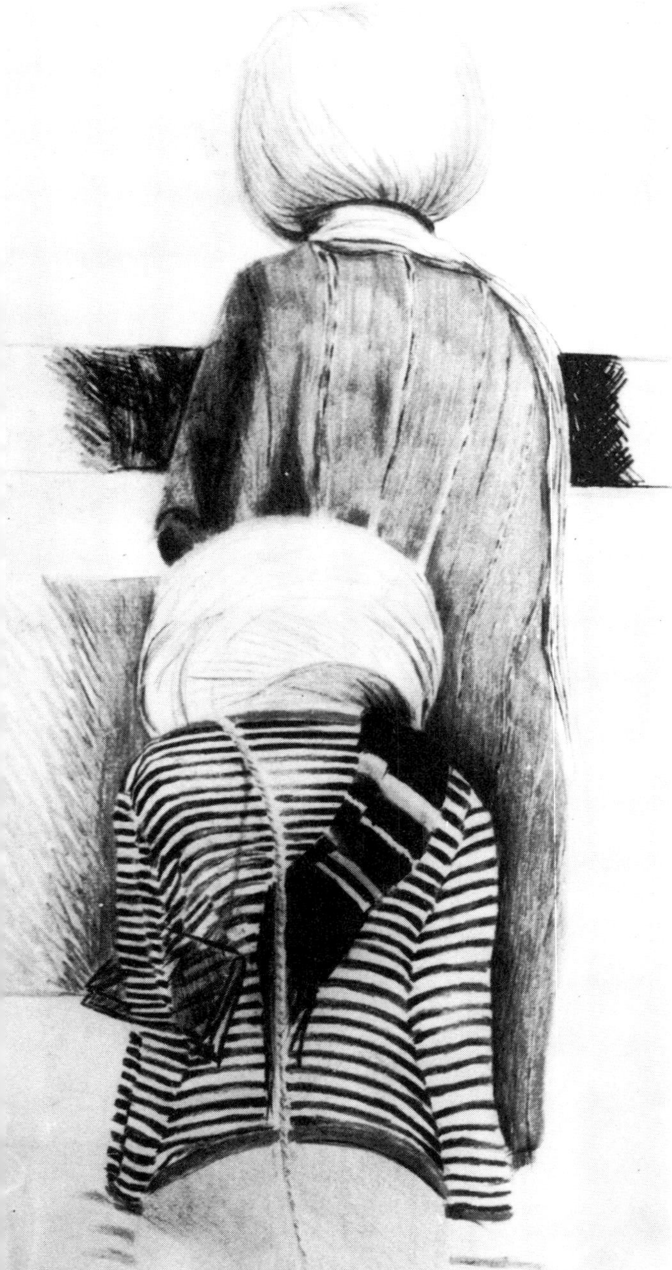

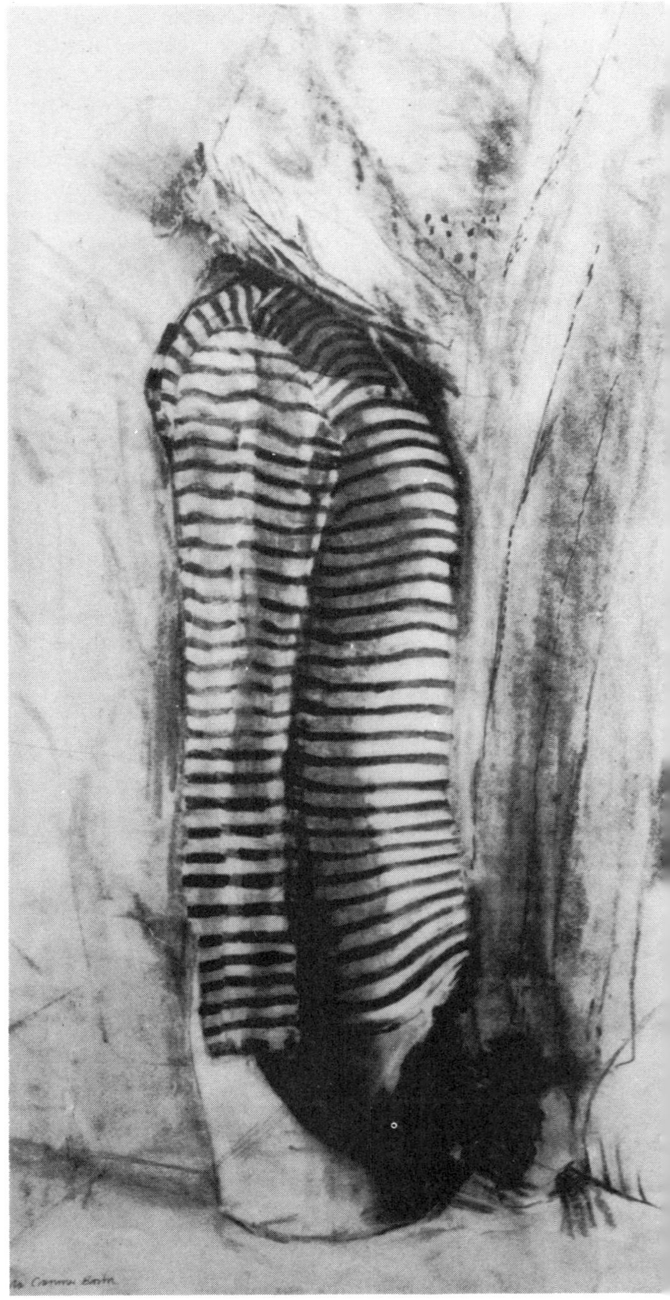

Drawings made by students from an idea used successfully in a school. Tailors dummies were given 'heads' of huge balls of string, then clothed and swathed in striped garments and material

formal or coding skills or combinations of these.

In the case of observational drawing the objects to be drawn are usually chosen or arranged in such a way as to emphasise either the formal qualities of line, tone and colour, or volume, space and sometimes movement. It is a creative and pleasurable activity to set up such situations. For example recently I have seen drawings where the children had been asked to give particular attention to the tonal range in the 'group' they were asked to draw. In order to help them they were given black paper and white chalk as well as charcoal. The fact that they were being put into a position where they had to work from dark to light, the opposite to looking from light to dark as is usual, heightened their perception of tonality.

The potential of the line to describe form is often the principal aim of a drawing activity. The swathing of objects or a figure in striped material, or the drawing of a linear object like a furled flag can make this point well. Even the basic shapes of the cone, cube and cylinder can be made fascinating (see illustration page 50) if their surfaces are treated in some way which enhances them. Inventiveness on the part of the teacher should be a stimulus to the children to create their own perceptual teasers. To play with actual line, tone and colour as well as volume and space and then to transform those actualities into a drawing would be a logical way to develop the manipulation of the components of drawing and the development of maximum flexibility and control of the skills of drawing.

CONCLUSION

The factors affecting the teaching of drawing are many and they are complex. Some of them affect the whole of learning, others just the learning of and through drawing. As teachers we must sensitise ourselves to all the common as well as the local influences. Adolescence and its characteristics, bearing in mind that this covers a long spell marked by many changes, is one major consideration. Other common factors that must be taken into account are the cultural and social background and mix of pupils and the outside influences brought to bear upon them in particular by peer-group value systems and the mass media. Adult attitudes to drawing education, as exhibited by parents and teachers of other subjects, has also to be taken into account as they affect many adolescents' approach to drawing and the confidence they both bring to it and gain from it. We have also to face historical and traditional beliefs about art and design and the practices and attitudes that have been engendered by them in others and in ourselves. The value systems of our society, especially as reflected in our education system, also have to be understood when faced with the problem of defining a conceptual structure upon which to base our teaching.

Other factors are concerned with the nature of drawing itself. What is drawing, what is its essence? Is it similar to other human thought and action or is it a unique way of thinking, of expression and of communication? What are the functions and the skills of drawing; is knowledge about drawing and facility in its use important and worthy of serious educational consideration?

The main uses of drawing have been described in this book in the belief that some of these functions have been neglected in art education over the last few decades, or at best have been ranked in a hierarchy. My own view is that this recent practice has done a disservice to drawing both in the eyes of our pupils and in the consciousness of the general public. In nineteenth-century England drawing was seen as an essential part of the educational 'core', a basic skill along with writing, reading and numeracy. There has been an insidious demoting of drawing by those who have real and fiscal power over the content of education, while, ironically, insights into ways of learning and teaching methodology have made enormous advances. The application of this knowledge has tended to be in primary education, and as far as subjects are concerned to literacy , to numeracy and to science. Money available for research has largely gone towards these subjects for reasons which are economic, social and political. The comparative neglect of the 'arts' subjects, however, is partially due to traditional reluctance on the part of the majority of teachers of these subjects to argue for them in social and political terms.

I regard the need to preserve drawing education for every child as a political issue. Informed 'reading', whether it be of speech, writing or imagery, is an important ingredient in the maintenance of personal choice, criticism and response. Knowledge of the human and technical processes whereby potent visual messages are made can only be acquired by practical experience of these processes. Such practice can in turn create understanding, record events and ideas and thus inform and effect change.

I have another, related, reason for believing in the necessity for drawing to remain and develop as a central ingredient in general education. Drawing creates a particular and private world of thought, feeling and action for the individual. This world cannot be replicated in any other activity for it allows for an exploration of ideas in tangible form which is essentially autonomous, flexible and examinable. This uniqueness of drawing has been described from two points of view. In the first drawing is seen as a way of knowing which does not deal in facts and testable skills but rather in a process of change where there is never a 'right' answer. It is concerned with a constant reconstruction of thought, feeling and reality. From the other viewpoint the uniqueness of drawing is that its symbolic, universal language transcends all others in communicating ideas.

This universality enables drawing to bring perceptions, thoughts and feelings together, it is cohesive. These two definitions are not necessarily contradictory. Drawing is able both to synthesise and to reconstruct, much depends on the circumstances in which the drawing is being made. To my mind the circumstances are made up of the *uses* for which the drawing is to be made and the level of competence, ie the drawer's ***skill*** as described earlier in this book.

My practical suggestions are that the teaching of drawing should be based on these two dimensions, through knowledge of drawing which describes, demonstrates and realises the functions of drawing, and through drawing which demonstrates and develops the skills of drawing. The sequence in which the components of these dimensions are introduced, and the pace, must be based on the individual teacher's assessment of the circumstances of the learner-participants.

School structures impose certain contraints and I have borne this in mind, especially when describing particular projects. Lack of adequate consecutive time, large teaching groups, the varying needs of both individuals within groups and between the groups to be taught within any one day, mitigate against many of the 'natural' aspects of pace and concentration we may feel are needed in the activity of drawing. In spite of these difficulties the essentials of teaching drawing can be sustained. If everyone concerned, teacher and taught, can understand and articulate the reason for the drawing in progress, that is not to say every detail of its characteristics, then good drawing education is taking place. When there is the confidence for a generous and honest exchange of views, criticism and advice to occur, drawing education has reached an enviable level.

I was shocked recently when an influential art educator declared that education in art was not necessarily the prerogative of every child, only those 'both gifted and interested'. I had assumed that every one in the field of art education believed themselves to be concerned with provoking interest and expertise in the subject. Furthermore I had assumed that teachers of drawing were concerned with promoting it as a tool of expression and communication for everyone, not only those exhibiting a certain talent or facility. Do we aim to make literate only the potential poet or novelist? Drawing is perhaps the most accessible of all the graphic arts and one of our earliest impulses is to engage in it. The drawings chosen to illustrate this book are almost without exception by young people who are not regarded as exceptionally outstanding at drawing. Their variety, efficiency, invention, wit and beauty is evidence of the potential universality of drawing as a form of knowing.

BIBLIOGRAPHY

Arnheim, R *Visual Thinking* Faber 1970

Barrett, Maurice *Art Education: a strategy for curriculum design* Heinemann 1979

Berger, John *Ways of Seeing* BBC 1972

Dubery, Fred and Willats, John *Drawing Systems* Studio Vista/Reinhold 1972

Eng, Helga *The Psychology of Child and Youth Drawing* RKP 1957

Goodnow, Jaqueline *Children's Drawing* Fontana/Open Books 1977

Green, Peter *Design Education* Batsford 1977

Gregory, R L *Eye and Brain* Faber 1969

Gregory, W L *The Intelligent Eye* Weidenfeld & Nicolson 1970

Hayes, Colin *Complete Guide to Painting and Drawing Techniques and Materials* BCA 1979

Lowenfeld and Brittain *Creative and Mental Growth* Collier Macmillan 1975

Maclure, Stewart *The History and Philosophy of Art Education* University of London Press 1970

Naylor, Gillian *The Bauhaus* Studio Vista 1964

Piaget, J *The Mechanism of Perception* RKP 1969

Rawson, Philip *Drawing* OUP 1969

Read, Herbert *Education Through Art* Faber 1958

Richardson, Marion *Art and the Child* London University Press 1948

Ruskin, John *The Elements of Drawing* Dover 1971

de Sausmarez, Maurice *The Dynamics of Visual Form* Studio Vista 1964

Viola, Willhelm 'Child Art' Longmans

'Learning through drawing' a booklet accompanying an exhibition of children's drawings pre-school to 18 years, organised by North Eastern Region of the Art Advisers Association

'Drawing: technique and purpose' catalogue to exhibition at Victoria and Albert Museum, Spring 1981

INDEX